Peter Robinson

Weak System Models for Distributed Agreement Problems

Peter Robinson

Weak System Models for Distributed Agreement Problems

Algorithms and Lower Bounds

Südwestdeutscher Verlag für Hochschulschriften

Impressum/Imprint (nur für Deutschland/only for Germany)
Bibliografische Information der Deutschen Nationalbibliothek: Die Deutsche Nationalbibliothek verzeichnet diese Publikation in der Deutschen Nationalbibliografie; detaillierte bibliografische Daten sind im Internet über http://dnb.d-nb.de abrufbar.
Alle in diesem Buch genannten Marken und Produktnamen unterliegen warenzeichen-, marken- oder patentrechtlichem Schutz bzw. sind Warenzeichen oder eingetragene Warenzeichen der jeweiligen Inhaber. Die Wiedergabe von Marken, Produktnamen, Gebrauchsnamen, Handelsnamen, Warenbezeichnungen u.s.w. in diesem Werk berechtigt auch ohne besondere Kennzeichnung nicht zu der Annahme, dass solche Namen im Sinne der Warenzeichen- und Markenschutzgesetzgebung als frei zu betrachten wären und daher von jedermann benutzt werden dürften.

Coverbild: www.ingimage.com

Verlag: Südwestdeutscher Verlag für Hochschulschriften GmbH & Co. KG
Dudweiler Landstr. 99, 66123 Saarbrücken, Deutschland
Telefon +49 681 37 20 271-1, Telefax +49 681 37 20 271-0
Email: info@svh-verlag.de

Approved by: Wien, TU, Diss., 2010

Herstellung in Deutschland:
Schaltungsdienst Lange o.H.G., Berlin
Books on Demand GmbH, Norderstedt
Reha GmbH, Saarbrücken
Amazon Distribution GmbH, Leipzig
ISBN: 978-3-8381-2729-3

Imprint (only for USA, GB)
Bibliographic information published by the Deutsche Nationalbibliothek: The Deutsche Nationalbibliothek lists this publication in the Deutsche Nationalbibliografie; detailed bibliographic data are available in the Internet at http://dnb.d-nb.de.
Any brand names and product names mentioned in this book are subject to trademark, brand or patent protection and are trademarks or registered trademarks of their respective holders. The use of brand names, product names, common names, trade names, product descriptions etc. even without a particular marking in this works is in no way to be construed to mean that such names may be regarded as unrestricted in respect of trademark and brand protection legislation and could thus be used by anyone.

Cover image: www.ingimage.com

Publisher: Südwestdeutscher Verlag für Hochschulschriften GmbH & Co. KG
Dudweiler Landstr. 99, 66123 Saarbrücken, Germany
Phone +49 681 37 20 271-1, Fax +49 681 37 20 271-0
Email: info@svh-verlag.de

Printed in the U.S.A.
Printed in the U.K. by (see last page)
ISBN: 978-3-8381-2729-3

Copyright © 2011 by the author and Südwestdeutscher Verlag für Hochschulschriften GmbH & Co. KG and licensors
All rights reserved. Saarbrücken 2011

This book[1] investigates various aspects of weak system models for agreement problems in fault-tolerant distributed computing. In Part I we provide an introduction to the context of this work, discuss related literature and describe the basic system assumptions.

In Part II of this book, we introduce the Asynchronous Bounded-Cycle (ABC) model, which is entirely time-free. In contrast to existing system models, the ABC model does not require explicit time-based synchrony bounds, but rather stipulates a graph-theoretic synchrony condition on the relative lengths of certain causal chains of messages in the space-time graph of a run. We compare the ABC model to other models in literature, in particular to the classic models by Dwork, Lynch, and Stockmeyer. Despite Byzantine failures, we show how to simulate lock-step rounds, and therefore make consensus solvable, and prove the correctness of a clock synchronization algorithm in the ABC model.

We then present the technically most involved result of this book: We prove that any algorithm working correctly in the partially synchronous Θ-Model by Le Lann and Schmid, also works correctly in the time-free ABC model. In the proof, we use a variant of Farkas' Theorem of Linear Inequalities and develop a non-standard cycle space on directed graphs in order to guarantee the existence of a certain message delay transformation for finite prefixes of runs. This shows that any time-free safety property satisfied by an algorithm in the Θ-Model also holds in the ABC model. By employing methods from point-set topology, we can extend this result to liveness properties.

In Part III, we shift our attention to the borderland between models where consensus is solvable and the purely asynchronous model. To this end, we look at the k-set agreement problem where processes need to decide on at most k distinct decision values. We introduce two very weak system models $\mathcal{M}^{\mathrm{anti}}$ and $\mathcal{M}^{\mathrm{sink}}$ and prove that consensus is impossible in these models. Nevertheless, we show that $(n-1)$-set agreement is solvable in $\mathcal{M}^{\mathrm{anti}}$ and $\mathcal{M}^{\mathrm{sink}}$, by providing algorithms that implement the weakest failure detector $\mathcal{L}$. We also discuss how models $\mathcal{M}^{\mathrm{anti}}$ and $\mathcal{M}^{\mathrm{sink}}$ relate to the f-source models by Aguilera et al. for solving consensus.

In the subsequent chapter, we present a novel failure detector $\mathcal{L}(k)$ that generalizes $\mathcal{L}$, and analyze an algorithm for solving k-set agreement with $\mathcal{L}(k)$, which works even in systems without unique process identifiers. Moreover, We explore the relationship between $\mathcal{L}(k)$ and existing failure detectors for k-set agreement. Some aspects of $\mathcal{L}(k)$ relating to anonymous systems are also discussed.

---

[1]This research has been supported by the Austrian Science Foundation (FWF) projects P17757 and P20529.

Next, we present a generic theorem that can be used to characterize the impossibility of achieving k-set agreement in various system models. This enables us to show that (Σ_k, Ω_k) is not sufficient for solving k-set agreement. Furthermore, we instantiate our theorem with a partially synchronous system model.

Finally, we consider the k-set agreement problem in round-based systems. First, we introduce a novel abstraction that encapsulates the perpetual synchrony of a run, the so called stable skeleton graph, which allows us to express the solvability power of a system via graph-theoretic properties. We then present an approximation algorithm where processes output an estimate of their respective component of the stable skeleton graph. We define a class of communication predicates $\mathcal{P}_{\text{srcs}}(k)$ in this framework, and show that $\mathcal{P}_{\text{srcs}}(k)$ tightly captures the amount of synchrony necessary for k-set agreement, as $(k-1)$-set agreement is impossible with $\mathcal{P}_{\text{srcs}}(k)$. Based on the stable skeleton approximation, we present an algorithm that solves k-set agreement when $\mathcal{P}_{\text{srcs}}(k)$ holds.

Contents

I. Introduction and Prerequisites

1. Introduction and Related Work   5
     1.1. Solvability of Distributed Computing Problems 7
     1.2. Failures and Consensus 8
     1.3. Exploring the Space of System Models 10
     1.4. The k-Set Agreement Problem 15
     1.5. Comparison of System Models 16
     1.6. Roadmap and List of Contributions 19

2. Basic System Assumptions   22
     2.1. Computation and Communication 22
     2.2. Failures 23
     2.3. Admissibility of Asynchronous Runs 24

II. Above Consensus Solvability

3. The ABC Model   27
     3.1. Synchrony in the ABC Model 28
     3.2. Knowledge Acquisition and Failure Detection 33
     3.3. Practical Aspects 35
     3.4. Comparing the ABC Model to Other System Models 36
         3.4.1. Relation to the classic partially synchronous model 36
         3.4.2. Relation to other partially synchronous models 40
     3.5. Discussion and Weaker Variants of the ABC Model 42

4. Byzantine Clock Synchronization · · · · · · · · · · · · · · · · · · 44
4.1. The Clock Synchronization Algorithm 45
4.1.1. Progress and Precision of Clocks 46
4.1.2. Clock Synchronization with Bounded Progress 51
4.2. Simulating Lock-Step Rounds 53
4.3. Discussion 55

5. Model Indistinguishability · 56
5.1. The Θ-Model 57
5.2. System Properties as Sets of Runs 58
5.3. Indistinguishability for Timing Independent Properties 60
5.3.1. Safety Properties 60
5.3.2. The Topology on Runs 61
5.4. Proof of the Main Theorem 63
5.4.1. Modeling Causality as a System of Linear Inequalities 63
5.4.2. The Cycle Space of the Execution Graph 69
5.5. Discussion 79

III. Below Consensus Solvability

6. Almost Asynchronous System Models · · · · · · · · · · · · · · · · · 81
6.1. Weak System Models for Set Agreement 81
6.1.1. The model $\mathcal{M}^{\mathrm{anti}}$ 82
6.1.2. Implementing $\mathcal{L}$ in Model $\mathcal{M}^{\mathrm{anti}}$ 83
6.1.3. The Model $\mathcal{M}^{\mathrm{sink}}$ 84
6.1.4. Implementing $\mathcal{L}$ in Model $\mathcal{M}^{\mathrm{sink}}$ 86
6.2. Consensus Impossibility 89
6.3. Comparing $\mathcal{M}^{\mathrm{sink}}$ to an f-Source Model 90
6.4. Discussion 91

7. The Generalized Loneliness Detector $\mathcal{L}(k)$ · · · · · · · · · · · · · 92
7.1. k-Set Agreement 92
7.2. Failure Detectors 93
7.3. Tightness of $\mathcal{L}(k)$ 94
7.4. Solving k-Set Agreement with $\mathcal{L}(k)$ 95

7.5. Relation between $\mathcal{L}(k)$ and $\mathcal{S}_{n-k+1}$	99
7.6. Relation between $\mathcal{L}(k)$ and Σ_k	102
7.7. $\mathcal{L}(k)$ in Anonymous Systems	106
7.8. Discussion	108

8. On the Impossibility of k-Set Agreement — 110
    8.1. T-Independence . . . 112
    8.2. The Impossibility Theorem . . . 113
    8.3. Applying Theorem 8.2.1 . . . 115
        8.3.1. The Partially Synchronous Case . . . 115
        8.3.2. Failure Detector (Σ_k, Ω_k) . . . 117
    8.4. Discussion . . . 121

9. A Communication Predicate for k-Set Agreement — 123
    9.1. The Round Model . . . 123
    9.2. Predicate $\mathcal{P}_{\mathrm{srcs}}(k)$ . . . 128
    9.3. Solving k-Set Agreement . . . 131
        9.3.1. Approximation of the Stable Skeleton Graph . . . 132
        9.3.2. k-Set Agreement . . . 138
    9.4. Discussion . . . 144

IV. Appendix

List of Figures   147

List of Algorithms   148

Bibliography   149

I

Introduction and Prerequisites

Chapter 1

Introduction and Related Work

> Luck favors the prepared mind.
>
> *(Louis Pasteur)*

> A distributed system is one in which the failure of a computer you didn't even know existed can render your own computer unusable.
>
> *(Leslie Lamport)*

A DISTRIBUTED SYSTEM IS a collection of processes that communicate with each other by sending messages over a network. In order to achieve a common goal, every process executes an instance of a distributed algorithm, which is modeled as a deterministic state machine, as proposed by Lynch and Fischer (1979). Taking into account the current, (locally) accessible state of the process and the received messages, the algorithm specifies what happens when a process takes a computing step, i.e., it determines which messages to send and what state transition to perform.

The so called *space-time diagram* provides an intuitive way to visualize the causality and communication between processes in a run of a distributed system. Figure 1.1 shows the space-time diagram of a run, for processes p_1, p_2, and p_3. Processes p_1 and p_2 communicate in a ping-pong like manner, by sending messages back and forth, and process p_3 periodically sends messages (m_1, m_2,...) to process p_1. Two computing steps are causally related, if one is reachable from the other in the space-time diagram without going backwards in time: For example, the step ϕ_3 at process p_1 causally depends on the steps ϕ_1 and ϕ_2, whereas steps ϕ_1 and ϕ_2 are causally unrelated.

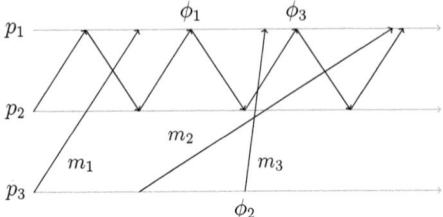

Figure 1.1.: The space-time diagram of a run of a distributed system.

While computer networks are without doubt the most prominent examples, distributed systems have meanwhile penetrated almost all areas of computing. The theory of distributed computing is also applied to diverse fields like VLSI systems on chip (e.g. Fuegger et al., 2006; Dielacher et al., 2009) and wireless ad hoc networks (e.g. Malpani et al., 2000; Wagner and Wattenhofer, 2007). Considering that distributed systems are frequently employed in safety-critical applications where the correct outcome of a distributed computation is a matter of life and death, it is indispensable to mathematically prove the correctness of distributed algorithms.

For the purpose of a formal analysis, a crucial first step is to find a suitable mathematical abstraction that hides the implementational details of the system while still retaining all of the important real world properties. The so called system model describes the behaviour of the system by mathematical axioms, the model assumptions, which determine the set of admissible runs of the model. For example, a model assumption could be that processes perform computing steps in round-robin order and no more than half of the processes malfunction. Depending on how well our observations correspond to the real system, the admissible runs of the model may or may not exactly match the runs that are actually possible in the system. The so called assumption coverage measures how well the model describes the real system. Care must be taken when choosing model assumptions, as a too restrictive model will be applicable to very few systems, whereas too relaxed assumptions might severely reduce the set of problems that can be solved in the model.

1.1. Solvability of Distributed Computing Problems

Given a problem P and a system model $\mathcal{M}$, the pivotal question in distributed computing is concerned with determining whether P is solvable in the model, i.e.,

is there any algorithm that solves problem P in model $\mathcal{M}$?

To be able to prove or disprove an instance of this rather generic question, we must first understand the meaning of the slightly more specific statement,

does a given algorithm A solve problem P in model $\mathcal{M}$?

As we have explained above, the set of admissible runs of model $\mathcal{M}$ consists of all *possible* runs where the model assumptions hold. In general, this set will also contain runs that are simply impossible when processes execute algorithm A. For example, inspecting the source code of algorithm A might reveal that two specific processes in fact never communicate; note that this is the case for processes p_2 and p_3 in Figure 1.1. We could therefore safely discard all runs where messages between those processes *are* sent, as they are irrelevant for our purpose. What we end up with is a set of "interesting runs" that is restricted in two ways: (a) by the model assumptions and (b) by the actual algorithm at hand.

Having identified the set of interesting runs, we will now take a closer look at the concept of a "distributed computing problem". Just like in the case of system models, the specification of a problem P induces a set of runs, which are precisely the runs where P holds. The above question, whether algorithm A solves problem P in model $\mathcal{M}$, can then be answered by simply comparing this set with the above set of interesting runs. That is, if every run that is generated by the algorithm and that is admissible in the model is also in the set of runs fulfilling the specification of the problem, then *algorithm A solves problem P in model $\mathcal{M}$*.[1] In other words, $\mathcal{M}$ is a sufficiently restrictive model and A is a cleverly-enough designed algorithm such that this combination produces only runs that satisfy the specification of P.

Returning to the first, more general question, i.e., whether there exists *any* algorithm that solves problem P in model $\mathcal{M}$, we could of course answer this question for a given algorithm by performing the above set-inclusion test. However, disproving the existence of any such algorithm, i.e., showing the impossibility of solving problem P in model $\mathcal{M}$ is considerably more involved, as we can no longer reason about the runs generated by *one*

---

[1] Note that we use the terms "run" and "execution" of an algorithm interchangeably.

specific algorithm. Instead, famous impossibility results like the consensus impossibility by Fischer et al. (1985) (described below), make use of an indirect argument: For the sake of a contradiction, assume that such an algorithm A exists. While we do not know the source code of this algorithm A, we might be able to make use of some (generic) properties that any algorithm that solves P must possess, simply because it solves P, in order to identify an appropriate run where algorithm A fails. If we can then show that this run where P does not hold is admissible in model $\mathcal{M}$, this of course yields a contradiction to our assumption that A solves problem P in $\mathcal{M}$, and therefore lets us conclude that no such algorithm can exist.

1.2. Failures and Consensus

Since distributed systems consist of multiple (independent) processes and communication links, a failure in some part of the system does not necessarily lead to an immediate failure of the entire system. Many distributed algorithms are therefore designed to be fault-tolerant, which means that they can cope with a certain amount of failures while still delivering the expected outcome. Essentially, failures can be classified either as link failures (see e.g. Schmid et al., 2009), where messages might be lost or corrupted, and process failures. When considering process failures, we can further distinguish between processes that fail by crashing, so called "benign failures", and processes that exhibit Byzantine behaviour. A process that crashes simply stops taking any computing steps and stays mute with respect to sending messages throughout the rest of the execution. Byzantine processes on the other hand were first introduced by Lamport et al. (1982) and capture the case where faulty processes not just stop working, but might also intentionally spread false information or attempt to corrupt other processes in order to jeopardize the successful operation of the algorithm. Apart from the kind of failures that can occur, the distribution of failures during a run is also important. For example, Biely and Hutle (2009) consider a model where processes might recover during a run, after exhibiting Byzantine behaviour.

A common requirement in a distributed system is the task of achieving agreement despite crashes of processes. In the pivotal consensus problem, which was formally defined by Pease et al. (1980) and originated from the transaction commit problem in distributed database systems (Dolev and Strong, 1982; Garcia-Molina, 1982; Lampson and Sturgis, 1979), all processes start out with (possibly distinct) input values from some domain. The specification of consensus then induces the set of runs where all non-faulty processes eventually decide on the same input value. In 1985, Fischer et al. showed in a seminal paper that there is no algorithm that solves the consensus problem in the asynchronous model, which has very weak model assumptions that are satisfied by many practical distributed systems of interest: Intuitively speaking, in runs of this model processes might crash and consecutive computing steps of a process can be separated by an arbitrarily long (finite, but unbounded) amount of time. Moreover, messages sent over communication links can suffer from unbounded (finite) transmission delays. Interestingly, the consensus impossibility holds even if we restrict the asynchronous model to the case where only a *single* process may crash per run, no matter how many other correct processes are part of the system. We will briefly sketch the main argument to emphasize the connection to the general impossibility argument described in the previous section. The impossibility proof of Fischer et al. (1985) exploits the fact that the asynchronous model assumptions are far too weak to implement a timeout mechanism or failure detection. That is, a process can never safely distinguish between the case where a message from some process p is still in transit, or in reality was never sent because p has previously crashed. Using this fact, the authors construct an infinite run where some correct processes never decide. Since in this run all messages are eventually delivered and every correct process takes infinitely many steps, it is admissible in the asynchronous model. As we will discuss below, circumventing this impossibility—by adding synchrony conditions or failure detectors to the asynchronous model—turned out to be one of the major research directions in distributed computing throughout the last decades.

Unsurprisingly, the amount of process failures directly influences the solvability power of a model. It was shown by Lamport et al. (1982) that consensus is solvable in the fully synchronous model only if less than a third of the processes are Byzantine. When considering crash failures and the wait-free failure assumption (see Herlihy, 1991), which allows all but one process to crash in a run, consensus, and in fact any other non-trivial agreement task, requires more restrictive synchrony assumptions compared to the case where only up to half of the processes might fail. Note that assumptions like wait-freedom can also be considered as progress conditions (Taubenfeld, 2010), since they specify under which conditions a process is expected to successfully complete a computation.

The probably first example of achieving agreement in the presence of link failures was introduced in Akkoyunlu et al. (1975) and called the "Two Generals Problem" by Gray (1978). In this problem a fortified city is besieged by two armies, each of which is lead by a general. In order to succeed, the two armies must both attack exactly at the same time; initially neither of them plans to attack. The generals can communicate by sending messengers to each other, which, however, might fail to deliver the message. That is, the only way general G_1 can be sure that his message has been delivered reliably, is by receiving some form of acknowledgement message from general G_2. To ensure the receipt of this acknowledgement, however, general G_2 in turn requires an acknowledgement from general G_1, and so forth. It can easily be shown that there is no finite protocol that allows the two generals to successfully coordinate an attack; see Akkoyunlu et al. (1975) and Halpern and Moses (1990) for a formal impossibility proof, and Schmid et al. (2009) for a refined argument.

1.3. Exploring the Space of System Models

The previous example shows that model assumptions can loosely be divided into failure assumptions and synchrony requirements. The former limits what kind of failures (e.g., Byzantine or benign) and what number (e.g., up to f faulty processes) can occur in runs admissible in the model.

Before discussing synchrony requirements in more detail, we need to clarify that we assume the existence of a discrete Newtonian timebase. That is, we assume a fictitious global clock such that every computing step is associated with a time-stamp that adheres to the usual causality assumptions. Note that this timebase is not necessarily in correspondence to real-time: In some system models, this fictitious clock might advance whenever a process has taken a computing step, disregarding how much actual real-time has passed between consecutive steps. Since causality between computing steps is fully captured by the happens-before relation introduced by Lamport (1978), and there is a compatible time-stamp assignment called logical time (Lamport, 1978; Mattern, 1992), this is indeed feasible. Very recently, the happens-before relation has been extended to non-asynchronous systems by Ben-Zvi and Moses (2010).

Synchrony requirements of a model essentially ensure that processes and communication network operate within some a priori given bounds with respect to this timebase. As we will see below, many existing models use synchrony requirements to (implicitly or explicitly) bound the so called end-to-end delays of messages, which spans the time interval starting at the computing step where a message is sent to the computing step when it is processed at the receiver.

The Synchronous Model

The space of system models for message passing systems is bounded by the fully (lock-step) synchronous model (see Lynch (1996, Chapter 2); Attiya and Welch (2004, Chapter 2)) on one hand, and by the aforementioned asynchronous model on the other hand. In the synchronous model, processes execute in so called lockstep rounds. A round consists of correct processes sending out messages to other processes and the reception and processing of these messages. Note that the round assumption by itself is not a real synchrony restriction, since we can structure the computing steps of processes into rounds even in the asynchronous model.[2] The distinguishing feature of the synchronous model is the fact that *all* messages that were sent at the beginning of the round are guaranteed to be delivered by the end of the round.

It is easy to see that the above mentioned consensus impossibility proof cannot be applied to this model: Operating in lockstep rounds guarantees reliable timeouts, in the sense that if a process does not receive the round-r message from process p by the end of round r, it can conclude with certainty that p has crashed.

Partially Synchronous Models

Now that we have roughly outlined the space of system models by introducing the synchronous and asynchronous models, we will explore its inner structure in more detail. When considering the consensus problem, it is well known that the model assumptions of the synchronous model are in fact unnecessarily strong. Several weaker models have been proposed where strict lockstep rounds are replaced by weaker synchrony assumptions.

The classic partially synchronous models introduced by Dolev et al. (1987); Dwork et al. (1988) and the semi-synchronous models (Ponzio and Strong, 1992; Attiya et al., 1994), incorporate a bound Φ on the relative speed of processes, in addition to a transmission delay bound Δ. All those models allow a process to timeout messages: The semi-synchronous models assume that local real-time clocks are available, in the sense that every process can query its local clock, while in the classic partially synchronous models computing steps (of the fastest process) are used as a timebase; in the latter case, using a spin-loop with loop-count Δ is sufficient for timing out the maximum message delay.

The seminal work of Dolev et al. (1987) contains the first systematic analysis of the impact of (un)favourable choices of system parameters on the solvability of the

---

[2]The beginning of a round is *not* necessarily a vertical cut in the timeline.

consensus problem. More specifically, Dolev et al. (1987) distinguish between point-to-point message transmission and broadcast communication, bounded vs. unbounded computing speed of processes and message delays, whether messages must be delivered in order, and the atomicity of the computing steps of processes. For example, Dolev et al. (1987) show that neither synchronous message transmissions nor synchronous computing steps alone are sufficient to circumvent the impossibility result of Fischer et al. (1985). Atomicity, which represents the power of a computing step, is often overlooked but nevertheless important. When speaking of atomicity here, we do not mean the granularity of computing steps with respect to real or logical time: Almost all existing distributed computing models assume that computing steps happen atomically and that steps are discrete, in the sense that they take zero time units.[3] Rather, atomicity refers to the ability of receiving and sending messages in the same computing step. At a first glance, this might appear to be a minor technicality, however, Dolev et al. (1987) show that consensus is still solvable when communication is broadcast-based and synchronous, despite asynchronous processes, *if* processes can send and receive within the same computing step.

One of the first partially synchronous models is the Archimedean model of Vitányi (1985), which assumes a bounded ratio $s \geqslant u/c$ on the minimum computing step time c and u, which is the maximum computing step time together with the transmission delay u. Analogously to the case of partially synchronous models described above, a process can timeout other processes by means of a local spin-loop with loop count s.

Probabilistic Synchrony Assumptions and Message Classification

While the partially synchronous models are close cousins to the synchronous model, the Finite Average Response time (FAR) model (see Fetzer and Schmid, 2004; Fetzer et al., 2005) is essentially a probabilistic assumption on top of the purely asynchronous model. More specifically, the properties of the FAR model are an unknown[4] lower bound for the computing step time, and an unknown finite average of the round-trip delays between any pair of correct processes. The latter condition allows runs where round-trip delays increase without bound, provided that there are sufficiently many short round-trips in between that amortize for the resulting increase of the average. Due to the computing step time lower bound, any process can implement a bounded-drift clock via a local

---

[3]See Moser (2009) for an in-depth analysis of allowing non-zero computing steps.

[4]The bound is "unknown" in the sense that it cannot be used in the code of the algorithm, while it is still available for the purpose of an analysis.

spin-loop, which allows to safely timeout messages by using the timeout values adapted at runtime.

The message-classification (MCM) model by Fetzer (1998) assumes that all received messages are correctly flagged as "slow" or "fast", depending on their message delays, with the requirement that the end-to-end delay of any slow message is more than twice as big as the end-to-end delay of any message flagged as fast. To prohibit flagging all messages as "slow", (Fetzer, 1998) assumes the existence of at least one correct process p that can eventually communicate bidirectionally with all correct processes via "fast" messages. Except for messages sent/received by this eventual bidirectional source p, the MCM model also allows message loss and even transient partitioning. Since the message classification assumption allows the implementation of a time-free timeout mechanism for "fast" round-trips (by means of local messages, sent from a process to itself, which are always delivered as "slow"), the MCM model makes consensus solvable.

Message-Driven Computation

When a process takes a computing step in any of the models we have seen so far, it removes zero or more messages from its receive buffer, and then runs the corresponding code of the algorithm that determines which messages to send. What we have not yet discussed is the enabling condition for such a computing step. System models can essentially be classified into time-driven and message-driven models. In time-driven system models like the partially synchronous models mentioned above, the computing steps of processes are triggered at specific points in time, usually determined by a local clock. In message-driven models, on the other hand, a process can only take a computing step when its receive buffer is nonempty, i.e., every computing step is triggered by the arrival of some message. The Θ-Model (see Le Lann and Schmid, 2003; Widder and Schmid, 2009) is a message-driven model where processes do not have access to hardware clocks. The synchrony assumption of the Θ-Model requires that the ratio between the maximum and minimum end-to-end delay of all messages currently in transit is, at all times, bounded by some possibly unknown constant Θ. Other similar message-driven models were used by Biely and Widder (2006, 2009) and Mattern (1989).

Failure Detectors

In contrast to the preceding models, failure detectors (Chandra and Toueg, 1996) provide a different approach for circumventing the impossibility result of Fischer et al. (1985).

Instead of requiring additional synchrony assumptions, the asynchronous model is augmented by giving every process access to an oracle that reveals information about the global state of the system. Chandra and Toueg (1996) introduce several failure detector classes of various strength and provide an algorithm that solves consensus in the asynchronous model augmented with the eventual weak failure detector $\Diamond \mathcal{W}$ or, equivalently, the leader election oracle Ω by Chandra et al. (1996), assuming that no more than half of the processes can fail by crashing. Obviously such failure detectors for consensus are not directly implementable in the asynchronous model, as this would contradict the impossibility of Fischer et al. (1985).

Since these failure detector models are "homogeneous" in the sense that the computing steps of processes and other system parameters are the same in all models, Chandra and Toueg (1996) introduce a "weaker than" relation on failure detectors, which we will discuss in more detail in Section 1.5.

The fact that the implementation of a failure detector requires some amount of synchrony in the underlying model, sparked the quest for the minimal synchrony requirements to implement failure detector Ω, which is sufficient for solving consensus (see Chandra et al., 1996). The first implementation of Ω was provided by Larrea et al. (2000) and was based on rather strong synchrony assumptions. The series of Weak Timely Link (WTL) models (Aguilera et al., 2001, 2008, 2004; Mostéfaoui and Raynal, 1999a; Anceaume et al., 2004; Malkhi et al., 2005; Hutle et al., 2006, 2009) can be viewed as a relaxation of the classic partially synchronous or semi-synchronous models, in the sense that only some communication links need to adhere to the bound on message delays. The latest WTL model of Hutle et al. (2006, 2009) requires just a single process p, a so called timely f-source, with f eventually timely links that connect p to a possibly changing set of f receiver processes. These models are less restrictive than the classic partially synchronous models, since communication over all other links in the system can be totally asynchronous.

Fernández and Raynal (2007, 2010) present the intermittent rotating f-star assumption that can be seen as a generalization (and a further weakening) of the above mentioned timely f-source assumption. Interestingly, the Ω implementation of Fernández and Raynal works even in runs where this star structure is not guaranteed during finite periods of time.

For shared memory systems, an implementation of Ω using a weak system assusmption was presented by Fernández et al. (2010).

Round Models

We have already described the structure of "rounds" when discussing the synchronous model. The round-by-round (RbR) failure detector framework of Gafni (1998) and the heard-of (HO) model of Charron-Bost and Schiper (2009) provide an elegant way for specifying predicates on the structure of rounds. More specifically, the communication predicates in the HO model limit the amount of lost communication in rounds, and therefore provide a way to ensure that certain synchrony conditions and failure conditions are met. Such a predicate could, for example, express that the system cannot be partitioned in any round. In every round r, the HO-set of a process p contains the ids of processes from which p has received a round, i.e., "has heard of" in round r. The round-by-round (RbR) failure detector framework of Gafni (1998), which is also applicable to shared memory systems, follows a complementary approach: Every process can query a local failure detector function D that returns a (not necessarily correct) list of suspected processes for the current round.

1.4. The k-Set Agreement Problem

While the consensus problem is indisputably the most important agreement problem in distributed computing, it is not always feasible in real systems. Especially in systems that need to function under wait-free failure assumptions, a temporary partitioning of the communication network might lead to scenarios where isolated parts of the system (must!) decide on different values.

Nevertheless, it is desirable that the processes still achieve agreement locally in every partition, i.e., if there are k partitions, there should be at most k different decisions. The so called k-set agreement problem introduced by Chaudhuri (1993) requires that in every run there are at most k different decision values among non-faulty processes. Clearly k-set agreement is a generalization of the consensus problem since 1-set agreement corresponds exactly to consensus. Furthermore, it was shown independently by Borowsky and Gafni (1993); Herlihy and Shavit (1993); Saks and Zaharoglou (2000) that k-set agreement is impossible in the asynchronous model if the possible number of failures in a system exceeds or is equal to k.[5] Analogously to consensus, matching failure detectors that make k-set agreement solvable in asynchronous systems have been discovered recently. For example, the loneliness detector (see Delporte-Gallet et al., 2008)

---
[5]Note that this perfectly matches the previously mentioned consensus impossibility in the asynchronous system with just 1 crash failure.

enables the weakest instance of k-set agreement, i.e., $(n-1)$-set agreement to be solved in asynchronous message passing systems. A detailed discussion of failure detectors for k-set agreement will be presented in Chapter 7.

A class of partially synchronous models that allow k-set agreement to be solved in shared-memory systems[6] have been proposed by Aguilera et al. (2009). These models generalize the partial synchrony assumptions of Dolev et al. (1987); Dwork et al. (1988) by assuming that only certain sets of processes need to behave synchronously as a whole, whereas individual processes might violate any synchrony bound. To the best of our knowledge, no weak system models for k-set agreement have been presented so far.

Other ways to circumvent the impossibility of k-set agreement (and hence also consensus) include the use of randomization (see e.g. Mostefaoui and Raynal, 2001) and weakening of the problem itself. An approach that restricts the problem at hand instead of augmenting the model is taken by Mostéfaoui et al. (2002), where a subset of allowed input vectors (i.e., the combinations of input values of processes) is identified such that k-set agreement is still solvable in asynchronous systems.

1.5. Comparison of System Models

One way to gain a deeper understanding of the space of system models that we have seen so far is to analyze the relative strength of models with respect to problem solvability. That is, we say that a model $\mathcal{M}_1$ is weaker than model $\mathcal{M}_2$ if every problem that can be solved with some algorithm in model $\mathcal{M}_1$ can also be solved with some (possibly distinct) algorithm in model $\mathcal{M}_2$. If also the opposite relation holds, we say that the models are equivalent, otherwise $\mathcal{M}_1$ is strictly weaker than $\mathcal{M}_2$. We have already argued, for example, why the synchronous model is strong enough to solve consensus, whereas the asynchronous model is not. Clearly, the asynchronous model is strictly weaker than the synchronous model.

An important point in our discussion is that system models that are equivalent with respect to problem solvability, do not necessarily share the same set of admissible runs. There are numerous cases of distinct models that are sufficient for solving consensus, despite the fact that neither set of admissible runs is a subset of the other. For example, the previously mentioned FAR model (Fetzer et al., 2005) and the MMR model (Mostefaoui et al., 2003) are an instance of such a case. Nevertheless, it makes sense to define an alternative comparison relation on models by using set-inclusion, where a model $\mathcal{M}_1$

---

[6]In this book we focus exclusively on message passing systems.

is weaker than model $\mathcal{M}_2$ if any run that is admissible in $\mathcal{M}_2$ is also admissible in $\mathcal{M}_1$. Compared to the relation on problem solvability defined above, this relation on the sets of admissible runs yields a more fine-grained order where the space of system models is a lattice, but not a linear order.

It is easy to see that being weaker with respect to inclusion of admissible runs also implies being weaker with respect to problem solvability power: Suppose that any run admissible in model $\mathcal{M}_1$ is admissible in model $\mathcal{M}_2$. Let A be an algorithm that solves problem P in model $\mathcal{M}_2$, i.e., the set of runs generated by A in model $\mathcal{M}_2$ is contained in the set of runs that satisfy the specification of P. By transitivity of set-inclusion it follows that P also holds for the set of runs generated by A in model $\mathcal{M}_1$, which means that any problem solvable in model $\mathcal{M}_1$ is also solvable in model $\mathcal{M}_2$. Note that this line of reasoning is only valid, if algorithm A "works" in model $\mathcal{M}_1$, in the sense that its operations are valid in $\mathcal{M}_1$. For example, algorithm A might require processes to periodically send out specific messages. Clearly such an algorithm would not be applicable in some message-driven model $\mathcal{M}_1$.

The comparison relation based on sets of admissible runs is therefore often useful when analyzing a class of closely related models that are all strong enough to solve a specific problem P. If the sets of admissible runs of these models are linearly ordered, we can use our relation to determine weaker models (w.r.t. this class!) to solve problem P. For example, the above approach was employed in the quest for the weakest model for solving consensus in the class of time-driven partially synchronous system models with weak timely links (WTL), as described in Section 1.3. Apart from its theoretical impact, finding weak system models is also of practical interest, since the implementation of such a system will be less costly and easier to achieve in general.

As we have mentioned previously, the WTL models do not directly strive to solve consensus, but rather implement the failure detector Ω, which in turn is sufficient for solving consensus. The leader oracle Ω outputs a single process id at every process and eventually stabilizes on the same correct id at every process. The reason why Ω was the target of choice for the WTL models is that Chandra et al. (1996) showed that Ω is the weakest failure detector where consensus is solvable. In more detail, Chandra et al. (1996) provide a generic reduction algorithm that, given any failure detector that solves consensus with some algorithm, implements Ω. In general, the possibility of transforming one failure detector into another, naturally defines a "weaker than" relation. Since it was shown by Jayanti and Toueg (2008) that there exists a weakest failure detector for every distributed computing problem, the transformation relation can also used to compare the hardness of distributed computing problems by comparing the corresponding weakest failure detectors.

1.6. Roadmap and List of Contributions

This book consists of three parts. In the remainder of Part I, we will establish some basic system assumptions in Chapter 2 and present a high level overview of the space of system models in Figure 1.2. The detailed content of Parts II and III is outlined below:

Part II

- In Chapter 3, we present the Asynchronous Bounded-Cycle (ABC) model, which is a novel time-free system model and also briefly discuss some practical aspects of the ABC model. Furthermore, we compare the ABC model to other already existing models, in particular to the classic model (Dwork et al., 1988) by Dwork, Lynch, and Stockmeyer.

- We then show how to simulate lock-step rounds in this model in Chapter 4 and solve bounded clock synchronization, despite Byzantine failures.

- In Chapter 5, we present the technically most involved result of this book: We prove that any algorithm working correctly in the partially synchronous Θ-Model also works correctly in our time-free ABC model. In the proof, we first apply a novel method for assigning certain message delays to asynchronous executions, which is based on a variant of Farkas' theorem of linear inequalities and a non-standard cycle space of graphs. Using methods from general topology, we then prove that the existence of this delay assignment implies model indistinguishability for time-free safety and liveness properties.

Part III

- We introduce two very weak system models $\mathcal{M}^{\text{anti}}$ and $\mathcal{M}^{\text{sink}}$ in Chapter 6 and prove that consensus is impossible in these models. We show how to solve $(n-1)$-set agreement in $\mathcal{M}^{\text{anti}}$ and $\mathcal{M}^{\text{sink}}$ by implementing the corresponding weakest failure detector. Analyzing how our model $\mathcal{M}^{\text{sink}}$ relates to the WTL models for solving consensus concludes Chapter 6.

- Chapter 7 introduces the generalized loneliness detector $\mathcal{L}(k)$, and shows how to solve k-set agreement without requiring unique process identifiers. Furthermore, we analyze how our failure detector $\mathcal{L}(k)$ relates to existing failure detectors for

k-set agreement and discuss its impact on the quest for the weakest failure detector in anonymous systems.

- We present a generic theorem in Chapter 8 that characterizes the impossibility of achieving k-set agreement in various settings. We apply Theorem 8.2.1 to show that failure detector (Σ_k, Ω_k) is too weak for k-set agreement and prove that k-set agreement is impossible in certain instances of the partially synchronous models of Dolev et al. (1987).

- In Chapter 9 we present a class of weak communication predicates $\mathcal{P}_{\text{srcs}}(k)$ and show how to use graph theory to express the inherent synchrony of a run. We then prove the correctness of a novel algorithm that solves k-set agreement by approximating the so called stable skeleton graph.

Parts of the results in this book are based on joint work with Martin Biely and Ulrich Schmid. See Robinson and Schmid (2008a,c,b, 2010), Biely et al. (2009a,b, 2010a), and Biely et al. (2011).

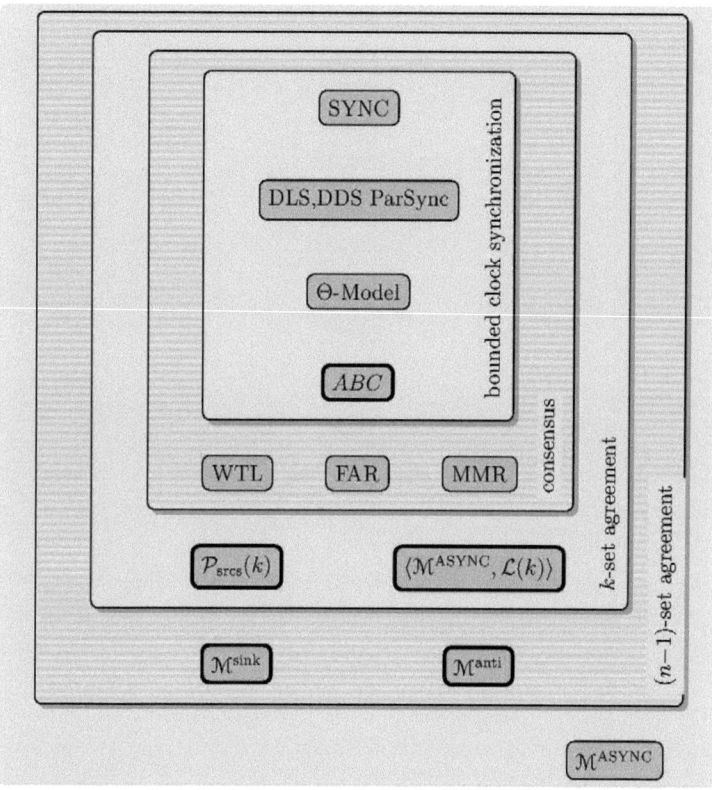

Figure 1.2.: The space of system models. The main focus of this book is an in-depth analysis of the emphasized (novel) models and the relationships between them. The vertical alignment shows the respective solvability power of models. For models that are equivalent in this aspect, the alignment reflects the strictness of their synchrony requirements. For example, while consensus is solvable in the ABC model and the Θ-Model, the ABC model requires less strict synchrony assumptions than the Θ-Model.

Chapter 2

Basic System Assumptions

IN THIS CHAPTER we will establish the system assumptions of model $\mathcal{M}^{\text{ASYNC}}$, which are relevant for all of the subsequently introduced models. It provides a formal basis for our journey through the space of system models of Figure 1.2 (Page 21).[1]

We will not, however, try to define a generic model and express the subsequent models as special instances. The reason why we choose a different approach here is that the underlying principles of some models discussed in this book are based on fundamentally different schools of thought and have little in common, apart from requiring the same set of the (very) basic system assumptions given below. For example, the ABC model (see Chapter 3) assumes message-driven computations and a synchrony assumption based on the structure of the space-time diagram (see Figure 1.1, Page 6), whereas the weak timely link model $\mathcal{M}^{\text{sink}}$ of Chapter 6 requires processes to perform partially synchronous computation in a time-driven manner. Trying to formulate such models as instances of a "greatest common denominator" model, would result in technically cumbersome proofs and obfuscate the essential properties of the respective model.

2.1. Computation and Communication

Since this book focuses on message passing systems, we consider a set Π of n distributed processes, connected by a point-to-point network with unbounded but finite transmission delays. Unless stated otherwise, this communication network corresponds to a fully con-

---

[1] Of course, these very basic system assumptions alone are insufficient for solving any non-trivial agreement problem, as we have already outlined in Chapter 1.

nected graph. We neither assume first-in-first-out (FIFO) message delivery guarantees nor the existence of an authentication service; we do assume, however, that a process knows the sender of a received message.

Every process executes an instance of a distributed algorithm and is modeled as a deterministic (and possibly infinite) state machine. Its local execution consists of a sequence of atomic, zero-time computing steps, each involving the reception of a set of messages In, a state transition, and the sending of zero or more messages to a subset of the processes in the system, denoted as Out. We assume that processes have access to a broadcast primitive, i.e., a process can send a message to all processes in the system in a single step. Note that, together with our assumptions that processes have unique identifiers, it is trivial to simulate point-to-point links on top of broadcast steps.

As we have pointed out in Section 1.3, there is a fundamental difference between models that use *time-driven* computation and the *message-driven* models. In the latter case, the set In contains exactly 1 message, i.e., every computing step of a process p is exclusively triggered by a single incoming message at p; process p's very first computing step is initiated by some external "wake-up message". To avoid the loss of messages, we assume that this very first step happens before p receives any message from another process.

For time-driven models, on the other hand, the set In can be of arbitrary finite size, meaning that processes can take steps independently of the communication within the network. To ease the analysis of algorithms in such time-driven models, we assume the existence of a *discrete global clock* T. The progress condition of T is specified by the model at hand, for now we can assume that T ticks whenever a correct process takes a step. Note that processes do *not* have access to T, which is merely a fictitious device.

2.2. Failures

We assume that among the n processes, at most f can be faulty. In this book, we are mainly concerned with crash failures and Byzantine processes.

If a process *crashes* (possibly within a step), it takes no further computing steps afterwards. We call a process *alive at time* t if it does not crash before or at time t.[2] Moreover, a process is alive in a time interval I when it is alive at every tick of T in I.

---

[2]Note that time t refers to the fictitious timebase of the discrete global clock T.

Definition 2.2.1. The *failure pattern* of a run α is a function $F : T \to 2^\Pi$ that outputs the set of crashed processes for a given time t. Moreover, we denote the set of faulty processes in the run as

$$F = \bigcup_{t \geqslant 0} F(t).$$

Since we assume that faulty processes do not recover, we have that

$$\forall t \geqslant 0 \colon F(t) \subseteq F(t+1).$$

The set of possible failure patterns is called *environment*. In Chapter 6, for example, we will consider any environment that allows up to $n - 1$ crashes, i.e., the *wait-free* environment (see Herlihy, 1991).

We conceptually distinguish between the reception of messages and the computing step where the process can react to this reception. In case of a correct receiver process, both refer to the same event. In case of a crash faulty or Byzantine receiver process, however, we separate the reception of a message, which is not under the control of the adversary but initiated by the network, from the processing of this message, which *is* under the adversary's control and hence arbitrary in the case of a faulty receiver. Consequently, even faulty processes eventually "receive" messages that are addressed to them.

In message-driven models we say that a message m sent by process p has been *processed* (or *executed*) by the correct process q, if a computing step triggered by m has been executed by q. Similarly, when considering time-driven computations, we say that m has been *received* by the (correct or faulty) process r if a receive event for m has occurred at r. Note that we do not define failure patterns for the Byzantine case, since Byzantine processes are considered to be faulty right from the start.

2.3. Admissibility of Asynchronous Runs

We can now specify necessary conditions for the admissibility of runs in our message passing systems. Depending on whether we are interested in message-driven or time-driven computations, either condition 4 or condition 5—which provide corresponding fairness conditions—need to hold. We have already discussed the atomicity of computing steps in Chapter 1. For message-driven computations, we always require that steps are atomic, since non-atomic steps where processes can *either* send or receive messages in a step (but not both), do not make sense in this setting.

Definition 2.3.1 (Admissibility in $\mathcal{M}^{\text{ASYNC}}$). A run is admissible in model $\mathcal{M}^{\text{ASYNC}}$ if all of the following conditions hold:

1. There are at most $f < n$ faulty processes.

2. Suppose that message m is sent by some correct process at time t. Then m is received, but not necessarily processed, by every (correct or faulty) recipient within finite time.

3. A message is only received at time t by process p if it was sent by some process q (and addressed to p) at some time $t' \leqslant t$.

4. (Message-driven only)
   - Computing steps are atomic.
   - If an infinite number of messages are sent to a correct process, it executes infinitely many computing steps.

5. (Time-driven only) A correct process executes infinitely many computing steps.

Our previous assumption that the global clock T ticks whenever a process takes a step, rules out so called "Zeno" behaviour, where processes can accelerate without bound and therefore might execute infinitely many computing steps before reaching some finite point in time. For instance, Sastry et al. (2009) present a system model that allows processes to accelerate and decelerate with respect to T, which corresponds to real time in the celerating model. Algorithms for this model explicitly require the exclusion of Zeno behaviour in order to work correctly.

Above Consensus Solvability

Chapter 3

The Asynchronous Bounded-Cycle Model

> I can't work without a model. I won't say I turn my back on nature ruthlessly in order to turn a study into a picture, arranging the colors, enlarging and simplifying; but in the matter of form I am too afraid of departing from the possible and the true.
>
> (Vincent van Gogh)

ADDING SYNCHRONY CONDITIONS, relating the occurrence times of certain events in a distributed system to each other, is the "classic" approach for circumventing impossibility results like Fischer et al. (1985) in fault-tolerant distributed computing.

Apart from the message classification model (Fetzer, 1998) and the MMR model (Mostefaoui et al., 2003), all other models introduced in Chapter 1 refer to individual message delays and/or computing step times, and most of them even involve explicit time bounds and system-wide global constraints. In this chapter we show how to add synchrony assumptions—sufficiently strong for implementing lock-step rounds, and hence for solving many important distributed computing problems like consensus—to the asynchronous model in a way that

- entirely avoids any reference to message delays and computing step times, and

- does not require system-wide constraints on communication patterns and network topology.

More specifically, our *Asynchronous Bounded-Cycle* (ABC) model bounds the ratio of the *number* of forward and backward messages in certain "relevant" cycles in the space-time diagram of an asynchronous execution only. Intuitively speaking, there is only one scenario that is admissible in the purely asynchronous model but not in the ABC model: A chain C_1 of k_1 consecutive messages, starting at process q and ending at p, that properly "spans" (i.e., causally covers, see Figure 3.1 on Page 31) another causal chain C_2 from q to p involving $k_2 \geqslant k_1 \Xi$ messages, for some model parameter $\Xi > 1$.

Consequently, individual message delays can be arbitrary, ranging from 0 to any finite value; they may even continuously increase. There is no relation at all between computing step times and/or message delays at processes that do not exchange messages; this also includes purely one-way communication ("isolated chains"). For processes that do exchange messages, message delays and step times in non-relevant cycles and isolated chains can also be arbitrary. Only *cumulative* delays of chains C_1 and C_2 in *relevant* cycles must yield the event order as shown in Figure 3.1. That is, the *sum* of the message delays along C_2 must not become so small that C_1 could span $k_1 \Xi$ or more messages in C_2. ABC algorithms can exploit the fact that this property allows to "time out" relevant message chains, and hence failure detection.

3.1. Synchrony in the ABC Model

In this section we will present a formal basis for the intuitive nature of the ABC model by stating the assumptions that need to hold, in addition to the ones required by $\mathcal{M}^{\text{ASYNC}}$ (see Definition 2.3.1 on Page 25).

The ABC model is a message-driven model, which means that the size of the set of received messages In per computing step, as defined in Chapter 2, is exactly 1. Throughout this chapter and Chapter 4, we assume that there are at most f Byzantine faulty processes in any admissible run, which means that these processes may deviate arbitrarily from the behavior of correct processes as described above. Since we distinguish between the reception and the actual processing of a message, there is a total order on the receive events at every process, no matter whether it is Byzantine or correct. Note that we do not assume anything about messages sent by Byzantine processes here, as they are usually unconstrained anyway.

Relevant Cycles and Causal Chains

The ABC model just adds one additional constraint on the admissible executions defined in Definition 2.3.1. It is based on the space-time diagram representing the happens-before relation (see Lamport, 1978), which captures the causal flow of information in an admissible execution. In order to properly include faulty processes, we just drop every message sent by a faulty process from the space-time diagram.[1] Note that a similar message dropping could be used for exempting certain messages, say, of some specific type or sent/received by some specific processes, from the ABC synchrony condition.

Definition 3.1.1 (Execution graph). The *execution graph* G_α is the digraph corresponding to the space-time diagram of an admissible execution α, with nodes $V(G_\alpha) = \Phi$ corresponding to the receive events in α, and edges reflecting the happens-before relation without its transitive closure: The pair (ϕ_i, ϕ_j) is in the edge relation $\rightarrow_\alpha \subseteq \Phi \times \Phi$ if and only if one of the following two conditions holds:

1. The receive event ϕ_i triggers a computing step where a message m is sent from correct process p to process q; event ϕ_j is the receive event of m at q. We call the edge $\phi_i \rightarrow_\alpha \phi_j$ *non-local edge* or simply *message* in G_α.

2. The events ϕ_i and ϕ_j both take place at the same processor p and there exists no event ϕ_k in α occurring at p with $i < k < j$. The edge $\phi_i \rightarrow_\alpha \phi_j$ is said to be a *local edge*.

We will simply write G and $\rightarrow$ instead of G_α and $\rightarrow_\alpha$ when α is clear from the context.[2]

In Figure 3.1 on Page 31, for example, the edge ℓ_1 that is incident to the messages m_1 and m_2 is a local edge, as it lies on the timeline of a single process.

Definition 3.1.2 (Causal chain and cycle). A *causal chain* $\phi_1 \rightarrow \cdots \rightarrow \phi_l$ is a directed path in the execution graph, which consists of messages and local edges. The *length of a causal chain* D is the number of non-local edges (i.e., messages) in D, denoted by $|D|$. A *cycle* Z in G is a subgraph of G that corresponds to a cycle in the undirected shadow graph of G.

---
[1] Recall that in this chapter we consider message-driven computation with zero-time atomic receive-compute-send steps only: every send event is triggered by some reception.
[2] Note that we will also consider execution graphs of *finite* prefixes of runs in Chapter 5.

Consider the causal chains

$$C_1 = m_6 m_7 m_8 m_9$$

and

$$C_2 = m_1 \ell_1 m_2 m_3 m_4 m_5 \ell_2$$

in the execution graph of Figure 3.1. Clearly we have $|C_1| = 4$ and $|C_2| = 5$, as the local edges ℓ_1 and ℓ_2 are not considered when calculating the length of a chain. To see why these chains form a "cycle" (as defined in Definition 3.1.2), first observe that C_1 and C_2 share two common vertices, namely the events ϕ_1 and ϕ_2. Now, taking a look at the undirected shadow graph depicted in Figure 3.2, we can see the *undirected* cycle $\bar{Z}$ that is spanned by the two disjoint paths that connect ϕ_1 and ϕ_2. The "cycle" Z that we are actually interested in is the subgraph in Figure 3.1 that is isomorphic to $\bar{Z}$, i.e.,

$$Z = m_6 m_7 m_8 m_9 \ell_2 m_5 m_4 m_3 m_2 \ell_1 m_1.$$

Until now, we have not at all considered the orientation of edges in the execution graph. Since messages cannot be sent backwards in time, every cycle consists of (at least) 2 disjoint causal chains that share common events. When starting out at some event in the cycle and traversing the entire cycle, we will inevitable traverse some edges oppositely to their orientation. If, for example, in Figure 3.1, we started at event ϕ_1 and continued to traverse along m_6, m_7, m_8, and m_9 we would move along the edges ℓ_2, m_5, ..., m_2, ℓ_1, m_1 in the opposite way, until we return to ϕ_1. That is, such a cycle traversal allows us to partition its edges into "forward" and "backward" edges, which is made explicit in the following definition:

Definition 3.1.3 (Relevant cycles). Let Z be a cycle in the execution graph, and partition the edges of Z into the class of *backward* edges $\hat{Z}^-$ and the class of *forward* edges $\hat{Z}^+$ as follows: Identically directed edges are in the same class, and

$$|Z^+| \leq |Z^-|, \tag{3.1}$$

where

$$Z^- \subseteq \hat{Z}^- \text{ and } Z^+ \subseteq \hat{Z}^+$$

are the restrictions of $\hat{Z}^-$ resp. $\hat{Z}^+$ to non-local edges (i.e. messages). The *orientation* of the cycle Z is the direction of the forward edges $\hat{Z}^+$, and Z is said to be a *relevant cycle* if all local edges are backward edges, i.e., if $\hat{Z}^+ = Z^+$; otherwise it is called *non-relevant*.

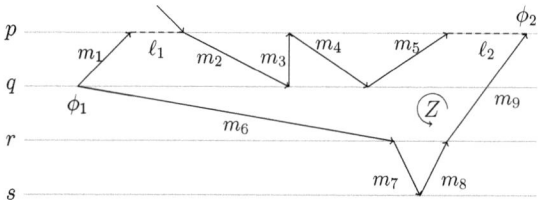

Figure 3.1.: A relevant cycle Z, where a causal chain $C_2 = m_1 \ell_1 m_2 \ldots m_5 \ell_2$ is spanned by the "slow" chain $C_1 = m_6 m_7 m_8 m_9$. Message m_3 has zero delay.

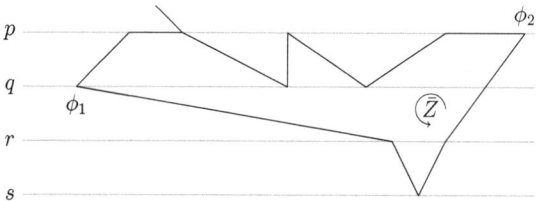

Figure 3.2.: This figure shows the undirected shadow graph of the execution graph of Figure 3.1. The two disjoint paths between events ϕ_1 and ϕ_2 span the cycle $\bar{Z}$.

Consider for example Figure 3.1: No matter how we traverse the cycle Z, we will end up with the unique partitioning

$$\{\{m_1, \ell_1, m_2, \ldots, m_5, \ell_2\}, \{m_6, \ldots, m_9\}\}$$

of the edges, w.r.t. their orientation. Property (3.1) states that the set of backward messages Z^- is never smaller than the set of forward messages Z^+. It follows that we have the following assignment for cycle Z:

$$\hat{Z}^- = \{m_1, \ell_1, m_2, \ldots, m_5, \ell_2\},$$
$$Z^- = \{m_1, m_2, \ldots, m_5\}, \text{ and}$$
$$Z^+ = \hat{Z}^+ = \{m_6, \ldots, m_9\}.$$

Since there are no local edges in $\hat{Z}^+$, cycle Z in Figure 3.1 is an example of a relevant cycle: Its cycle orientation is opposite to the direction of all local edges, and the backward messages are traversed oppositely with respect to their direction when traversing the cycle according to this orientation. In Figure 3.5 (Page 34) on the other hand, the order of events ϕ and ψ make the cycle N non-relevant, as the local edge between ϕ and ψ is a forward edge. The reason why we choose to call some specific cycles "relevant" and others "non-relevant" will become apparent in Section 3.2, where we will see that relevant cycles allow processes to perform failure detection.

Bear in mind, however, that labelling an edge in a cycle as a "forward" or "backward" edge is only of local significance. For example, in Figure 3.3, the forward message e in cycle X is actually a backward message in cycle Y (i.e., $e \in X^+$ and $e \in Y^-$).

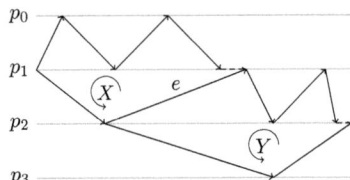

Figure 3.3.: An execution graph containing relevant cycles X, Y, and the combined cycle $X \oplus Y$, consisting of all edges except the oppositely oriented edge e.

Definition 3.1.4 (ABC synchrony condition). Let $\Xi > 1$ be a given rational number, and let G be the execution graph of an execution α where processes perform message-driven computation. Then α is *admissible in the ABC model* if α is admissible in $\mathcal{M}^{\text{ASYNC}}$ (see Definition 2.3.1) and, for every relevant cycle Z in G, we have that

$$\frac{|Z^-|}{|Z^+|} < \Xi. \tag{3.2}$$

Intuitively speaking, (3.2) ensures that the ratio of backward messages (i.e. edges in Z^-) to forward messages is bounded in relevant cycles. Returning to the example in Figure 3.1, this execution graph would be admissible in an ABC model with

$$\Xi > \frac{5}{4},$$

since $|Z^-| = 5$ and $|Z^+| = 4$, and Z is the only relevant cycle here.

Apart from the above condition, there is no other constraint in the ABC model with respect to the purely asynchronous model: Only the ratio of the *number* of backward vs. forward messages in relevant cycles is constrained. There is no system-wide assumption that restricts the behavior of processes that *do not* communicate with each other, no delay constraints whatsoever are put on individual messages, and messages in non-relevant cycles and isolated chains are totally unconstrained.

3.2. Knowledge Acquisition and Failure Detection

Despite the absence of explicit synchrony bounds, we will prove in Chapter 4 that the ABC synchrony condition is sufficient for simulating lock-step rounds, and hence for solving e.g. consensus by means of any synchronous consensus algorithm.

Informally, this is true because condition (3.2) facilitates "timing out" message chains and hence failure detection[3]: For example, a correct process p could use its knowledge of Ξ to timeout a crashed process p_{slow}, by communicating in a ping-pong-like manner with a correct process p_{fast}. That is, process p sends a message to p_{fast} which immediately sends back a reply. This in turn causes p to send another message to p_{fast} and so forth. Suppose that, as depicted in Figure 3.4, p has initially broadcast a message to p_{slow} and p_{fast}. Assume that, after $\Xi = 2$ ping-pong sequences (i.e., a causal chain of length 2Ξ) between p and p_{fast}, no reply message from p_{slow} has yet arrived at p. If this reply message arrived at p at some point later on, then the receive event of this message would close a relevant cycle and thereby violate the synchrony assumption (3.2). Hence, in computing step ψ, process p can safely conclude that p_{slow} must have crashed. Note that the ABC synchrony condition is used indirectly here: The absence of a reply message allows p to timeout p_{slow}, because its later arrival would violate the ABC synchrony condition.

It is instructive to consider what happens if the message from p_{slow} arrives before the event ψ occurs, as shown in Figure 3.5. In that case, ψ closes a non-relevant cycle—

---
[3]Note that in this example we consider only crash-faulty processes rather than Byzantine behaviour.

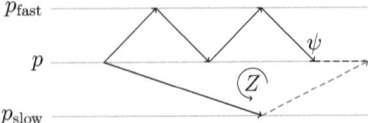

Figure 3.4.: If a reply message arrived from p_{slow} after event ψ, there would be a relevant cycle Z where $\frac{|Z-|}{|Z+|} = \frac{4}{2}$.

the local edge (ϕ, ψ) between the receive events ϕ and ψ has the same direction as the orientation of the cycle N. In sharp contrast to the situation depicted in Figure 3.4, however, p does not gain any new information about p_{fast} in the computing step ψ closing the resulting non-relevant cycle: Process p has already inferred that p_{slow} is still alive in the previous computing step ϕ (which actually closes a smaller relevant cycle!). Therefore, non-relevant cycles are indeed irrelevant for an ABC algorithm.

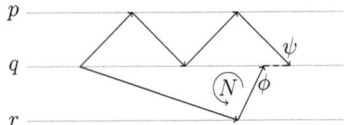

Figure 3.5.: Example of a non-relevant cycle N.

At a first glance, the above examples suggest that we could simplify the ABC synchrony condition by stating certain order properties on fast resp. slow message chains, i.e., by considering relevant cycles that consist of exactly one fast and one slow message chain only. However, this would unnecessarily restrict the way algorithms could exploit the ABC synchrony condition: It may well be the case that some clever (not-yet discovered) algorithm could infer synchrony information from more complex message patterns. Moreover, in the case of Byzantine failures, there can be cycles involving multiple overlapping message chains. For example, the correctness proof of Algorithm 1 shown in Figure 4.1 would no longer work with this simplified assumption, as the cycle consists of 3 separate message chains:

$$\phi_0 \to \psi_2,\ \psi_1 \to \phi'',\ \text{and}\ \phi_0 \to \phi''.$$

This makes it necessary to state Definition 3.1.4 in terms of general cycles, as we did, rather than via causal chains.

3.3. Practical Aspects

Since the ABC model shares many features with the Θ-Model, most of the applicability and model coverage aspects discussed by Widder and Schmid (2009) apply a forteriori to the ABC model. In particular, as a message-driven model, the ABC model suffers from the problem that the entire system may become mute in case of excessive message loss and/or partitioning, and that the overhead of continuously sending messages may become significant. Although there are ways of mitigating these problems, they cannot be ruled out completely. At the same time, ABC algorithms are easily portable and benefit from the ABC model's good coverage in real systems.

Moreover, the non-global scope of the ABC synchrony condition (3.2), which only constrains messages in relevant cycles on a per-cycle basis, makes the ABC model also applicable to in systems that cannot be modeled by the existing partially synchronous models. Consider a formation of spacecraft, for example, where clusters of spacecraft continuously move away from each other but stay close within a cluster: If an algorithm generates only message chains that span multiple clusters in relevant cycles, a properly chosen ABC synchrony condition in the corresponding execution graph will always be maintained. No existing partially synchronous model can adequately model such systems: The DLS Model (Dwork et al., 1988), the Archimedean Model (Vitányi, 1984) and the WTL Models (Aguilera et al., 2004; Malkhi et al., 2005; Hutle et al., 2006) assume some (possibly unknown) global delay bound for all timely messages. The Θ-Model (Widder and Schmid, 2009), on the other hand, suffers from the problem that *all* messages simultaneously in transit within the whole system must obey the global delay ratio Θ. Somewhat an exception is the FAR-Model, which does not require any correlation between the delays of messages exchanged by different processes; it fails to model the above example, however, because of the ever-growing delays.

Interestingly, the ABC model is also a promising candidate for modeling distributed algorithms in *very large scale integration* (VLSI) circuits:[4] Due to continuously shrinking feature sizes and increasing clock speeds, today's deep sub-micron VLSI have much in common with loosely-coupled asynchronous distributed systems studied in distributed

---
[4]See e.g. the Dagstuhl seminar *Fault-Tolerant Distributed Algorithms in VLSI Chips* organized by (Charron-Bost et al., 2009).

computing for decades, see e.g. (Sutherland and Ebergen, 2002; Ebergen, 1991). Given that the delays observed in a particular chip depend heavily on the VLSI implementation technology, as well as on the actual place-and-route of the components and wires, it is definitely sub-optimal to compile time values into a distributed algorithm here — in particular, when those values affect its internal structure (message-buffer sizes, for example): Re-using such an algorithm in conjunction with a different implementation technology or within a different application would be difficult.

By contrast, when an ABC algorithm is used in the VLSI context, there is a very good chance that the algorithm can be re-used without a change. In particular, when a design is migrated to a, say, faster implementation technology, both minimum and maximum delay paths are usually sped up in a similar way. Hence, the algorithm's Ξ is likely to continue to hold. Similarly, if an ABC algorithm is employed within a different VLSI application, one can usually guarantee its Ξ by setting suitable constraints during place-and-route. Thanks to the ABC model's weak properties, these constraints concern *cumulative* delays, and timing *ratios* only. They are hence much easier to satisfy than explicit timing constraints put on individual components and wires.

3.4. Comparing the ABC Model to Other System Models

In this section, we relate the ABC model to some of the existing partially synchronous models described in Section 1.3.

The fact that we will primarily discuss aspects where the ABC model surpasses alternative models should not be taken as a claim of general superiority, however: A fair model comparison is difficult and also highly application-dependent; it almost always leads to the conclusion that any two models are incomparable, in the sense that model A is better than B in aspect X but worse in aspect Y, cp. Widder and Schmid (2009). We start with a brief account of the major features of those models.

3.4.1. Relation to the classic partially synchronous model

In this section, we relate the ABC model to the classic partially synchronous model, to which we will refer to as DLS model from now on. Note that we consider only the *perpetual* variants of the DLS model here, i.e., for the global stabilization time t_{GST}

we have $t_{\text{GST}} = 0.5$ introduced by Dwork et al. (1988). The model DLS stipulates a bound Φ on relative computing speeds and a bound Δ on message delays, relative to an (external) discrete "global clock", which ticks whenever a process takes a step: During Φ ticks of the global clock, every process takes at least one step, and if a message m was sent at time k to a process p that subsequently performs a receive step at or after time $k + \Delta$, p is guaranteed to receive m.

First of all, we note that the ABC model and DLS are equivalent in terms of solvability of timing independent problems in fully connected networks. In Widder and Schmid (2009), it was shown that the Θ-Model and DLS are equivalent in this regard: Since the synchrony parameters Φ, Δ of the DLS model imply bounded (and non-zero) end-to-end delays, any Θ-algorithm can be run in a DLS system if $\Theta = \Theta(\Phi, \Delta)$ is chosen sufficiently large. Conversely, using the lock-step round simulation for the Θ-Model provides a "perfect" DLS system ($\Phi = 1$ and $\Delta = 0$), which obviously allows to execute any DLS algorithm atop of it. The claimed equivalence thus follows from the model indistinguishability of the ABC model and the Θ-Model established in Section 5.

This problem equivalence does not imply that the models are indeed equivalent, however. First, as shown below, there are problems that can be solved in the ABC model but not in DLS in the case of not fully connected networks and/or distributed algorithms where processes communicate only with a subset of the other processes. Moreover, whereas we can choose Ξ such that every execution of a message-driven algorithm in DLS with Φ, Δ is also admissible in the ABC model for some $\Xi > \Theta(\Phi, \Delta)$, we can even conclude from $\mathcal{M}_{\text{ABC}} \supset \mathcal{M}_\Theta$ that some ABC executions cannot be modeled in DLS. In fact, it has been shown by Widder and Schmid (2009) that there are Θ-executions that cannot be modeled in DLS.

To investigate this issue also from a different perspective, it is instructive to embed the ABC model in the taxonomy of partially synchronous models introduced by Dolev et al. (1987): In this seminal work, the exact border between consensus solvability and impossibility has been determined. It distinguishes whether (c) communication is synchronous (Δ holds) or asynchronous, whether (p) processes are synchronous (Φ holds) or asynchronous, whether (s) steps are atomic (send+receive in a single step) or non-atomic (separate send and receive steps), whether (b) send steps can broadcast or only unicast, and whether (m) message delivery is (globally) FIFO ordered or out-of-order.

---

[5]Some issues related to the eventual variants ($t_{\text{GST}} > 0$) were discussed in Section 3.5. A detailed relation of all variants of DLS models to the corresponding variants of the Θ-Model was presented in (Widder and Schmid, 2009).

We will argue below that, within this taxonomy, the ABC model model must be mapped to the case of asynchronous communication, asynchronous processes, atomic steps, broadcast send and out-of-oder delivery. Using the corresponding "binary encoding" ($c=0, p=0, s=1, b=1, m=0$) of Dolev et al. (1987, Table 1), it turns out that consensus is not solvable in the resulting DLS model. The apparent contradiction to the solvability of consensus in the ABC model is due to the ABC synchrony condition, which (weakly) restricts the asynchrony of processes and communication. Since this restriction is not expressible in the taxonomy of Dolev et al. (1987), the ABC model must be "over-approximated" by totally asynchronous processes and communication here.

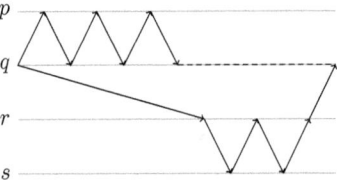

Figure 3.6.: A relevant cycle, valid for any $\Xi > 1$. Note that r takes no step while p and q can make progress only bounded by $|Z^-|$.

Asynchronous communication and asynchronous processes:

Consider a 2-player game where the Prover first chooses Ξ and the Adversary, knowing Ξ, chooses a pair (Φ, Δ). Finally, the Prover has to choose an execution satisfying (3.2) for Ξ; the Prover wins iff this execution violates the adversary-chosen parameters (Φ, Δ). The Prover has a winning strategy: It suffices to choose any execution containing a relevant cycle as shown in Figure 3.6, which respects (3.2) but lets $|Z^-|$ be greater than both Φ and Δ: While the (slow) message from q to r is in transit, process q executes more than Δ steps. Moreover, neither process r nor s execute a step during the more than Φ steps of q. As a consequence, both communication and processes must be considered asynchronous ($c=0, p=0$).

Atomic steps and broadcast:

Whereas it is clear that out-of-order delivery ($m=0$) makes it more difficult to solve problems, one may be wondering whether the "favorable" choices $s=1$ and $b=1$, rather than the ABC synchrony condition, make consensus solvable in the ABC model. Dolev et al. (1987, Table 1) reveals that this is not the case, however: All the entries corresponding to $p=0, c=0, m=0$ are the same (consensus impossible), irrespectively of the choice of b and s. And indeed, the assumption of atomic send+receive steps with broadcast in the ABC model's definition in Section 3.1 is just a simplifying abstraction: Every non-atomic unicast execution can be mapped to a causally equivalent atomic send+receive+broadcast step execution with appropriately adjusted end-to-end delays. The ABC model can hence also be used for making classic distributed algorithms results applicable to non-atomic models like the Real-Time Model introduced by Moser and Schmid (2006).

Another major difference between DLS and the ABC model results from the cumulative and non-global character of the ABC synchrony condition. Since (3.2) needs to hold only in relevant cycles, which are in fact defined by the message patterns of the specific algorithm employed, the ABC model is particularly suitable for modeling systems with not fully connected communication graphs: For choosing Ξ, only the cumulative end-to-end delay ratio over certain paths counts.

Consider the execution shown in Figure 3.7, for example, which corresponds to a system where process q exchanges messages directly with p (over a 1-hop path P_{qpq}), and indirectly with s (over a 2-hop path P_{qrsrq} via r). As long as the sum of the delays along P_{qrsrq} is less than the cumulative delay of Ξ instances of P_{qpq}, the individual delays along the links between q, r and r, s are totally irrelevant. In the VLSI context, for example, this gives more flexibility for place-and-route, as well as some robustness against dynamic delay variations. By contrast, in DLS, very conservative values of Φ, Δ would be needed to achieve a comparable flexibility; obviously, this would considerably degrade the achievable performance system-wide.

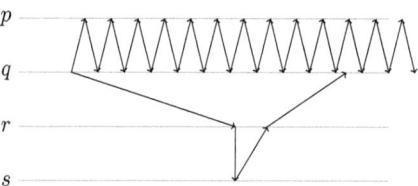

Figure 3.7.: The long delay on the link between q and r is compensated by the fast delay on the link between r and s.

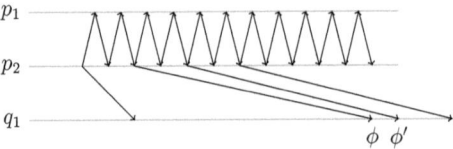

Figure 3.8.: A system implementing bounded-size FIFO channels. If the order of ϕ and ϕ' changed, there would be a relevant cycle violating (3.2) if $\Xi = 4$.

In the case of not fully connected networks, there are even situations which cannot be modeled in DLS at all. Consider the message-pattern given in Figure 3.8 in a system with $\Xi = 4$, for example: The ABC synchrony condition ensures FIFO order of the messages sent from p_2 to q_1, even when their delay is unbounded (and may even continuously grow, as e.g. in a formation of fixed-constellation clusters of spacecraft that move away from each other): If there was a reordering of ϕ and ϕ', a relevant cycle with $\Xi = 5$ would be formed, which is not admissible for $\Xi = 4$ and hence cannot occur. Note that processes p_1, p_2 make unbounded progress while a message to q_1 is in transit here. Hence, as in the example of Figure 3.6 mentioned before, the problem cannot be solved in DLS. Clearly, such message ordering capabilities are very useful in practice, e.g., for implementing stable identifiers, bounded-message size, single source FIFOs etc.

3.4.2. Relation to other partially synchronous models

In this section, we will briefly relate the ABC model to the remaining partially synchronous models MCM and MMR listed in Section 1.3.

Whereas most existing partially synchronous models refer to message delays and computing step times, the ABC model only constrains the ratio of the number of backward vs. forward messages in relevant cycles. Moreover, the ABC model neither assumes any relation between computing step times and message delays, nor real-time clocks, hence is less constraining than the models considered in Section 3.4.1. Note that this is also true for the FAR-Model by Fetzer et al. (2005), which requires a bounded-speed clock and hence introduces some (weak) dependency between average message delays and computing steps as well. The only exceptions are the Θ-Model, which constrains the maximal/minimal end-to-end delay ratio, the MCM model by Fetzer (1998) that assumes a classification of received messages in "slow" and "fast" ones, and the MMR model of Mostefaoui et al. (2003), which restricts the message order in round-trip communication patterns.

Like the ABC model, the MCM model is totally time-free, yet allows to reliably timeout certain messages. However, whereas the MCM uses local "slow" messages to timeout a round-trip of "fast" ones, the ABC model uses "fast" message chains to timeout "slow" ones[6]. The message classification assumption is hence more demanding than the ABC condition, since no two messages with delay ratio in the interval $(1,2]$ may ever be in transit simultaneously (unless they are both "slow").

The MMR model by Mostefaoui et al. (2003) also applies to systems with at most f process crash failures. It assumes that, in every round-trip of process p_i with all its peers, there is a fixed set of processes Q_i the responses of which are among the first $n-f$ responses received by p_i. This property turned out to be sufficient for implementing the eventually strong failure detector $\diamond S$ and, hence, to solve consensus.

Like the ABC condition, the MMR condition enforces a certain order of events. Although this condition cannot be expressed explicitly in the ABC model, it can be interpreted as a special instance of the (undefined[7]) situation $\Xi = 1$ for certain messages. Due to its order-based synchrony condition, the MMR model shares several advantages of the ABC; on the down side, it is restricted to a specific communication pattern and has a quite demanding synchrony requirement (albeit for certain messages only). Moreover, the ABC model is superior w.r.t. solvability of problems, since the MMR model does not allow to reliably timeout messages. It is hence impossible to implement uniform lock-step rounds, for example: If a process q sends a round message to p and then immediately crashes, p cannot distinguish this from the scenario where q has crashed before sending the round message. Consequently, neither Lemma 4.1.6, which gives a bound on the failure detection time, nor the bounded progress condition in Theorem 4.1.11 could be derived in the MMR model. Actually, the same is true for any model that does not provide stronger synchrony properties than provided by a perfect failure detector, i.e., for any model where the Strongly Dependent Decision Problem cannot be solved (see Charron-Bost et al., 2000).

A particularly attractive property of the ABC model is its ability to deal with unbounded message delays. Among the existing partially synchronous models, this is also true for the MCM model, the MMR model, the FAR-Model and the dynamic Θ-Model. The FAR-Model actually surpasses the ABC model here, in the sense that it does not

---

[6]Note that, in contrast to the MCM model, in the ABC model there is no global classification of messages into "fast" and "slow" messages, as a "fast" (i.e. *backward*, see Definition 3.1.3) message in one cycle Z might actually be a "slow" (i.e. *forward*) message in another cycle Y.

[7]Since this would make the definition of forward and backward edges (and hence of relevant and irrelevant cycles) superfluous, the ABC model does not allow $\Xi = 1$.

require any correlation between the delays of messages exchanged by different processes. On the other hand, the FAR-Model is inferior to the ABC model due to its requirement of finite average message delays, which rules out continuously growing delays (occurring e.g. in a formation of spacecraft that continuously move away from each other). The remaining partially synchronous models also allow growing delays, although all message delays must change roughly at the same rate. By contrast, as already mentioned in Section 3.4.1, the ABC model does not force unrelated messages to meet any constraints, and even allows messages with zero delay.

The partially synchronous model $\mathcal{M}_*$ of Sastry et al. (2009) distinguishes itself from existing models by considering so called "celerating" environments, where processes can arbitrarily accelerate or decelerate. Sastry et al. (2009) show how to implement the eventually perfect failure detector in $\mathcal{M}_*$ by using a bichronal clock, which allows processes to perform failure detection by combining a real-time clock and a logical clock. In contrast to the partially synchronous models of Dolev et al. (1987) and Dwork et al. (1988), model $\mathcal{M}_*$ separates the bound on message delays from the bound on the computing speed of processes, i.e., processes might speed up (or slow down) while message delays remain the same. Model $\mathcal{M}_*$ is not directly comparable to the ABC model, as the message-driven assumption always requires process and message transmissions to accelerate (decelerate) simultaneously.

3.5. Discussion and Weaker Variants of the ABC Model

There are various interesting ways how the synchrony condition (3.2) can be weakened. Analogously to Dwork et al. (1988) and Widder and Schmid (2009), it is possible to define 4 variants of the ABC model:

- ABC model: Ξ is known and holds perpetually (the model introduced in Section 3.1)

- ?ABC model: Ξ is unknown and holds perpetually

- $\diamond$ABC model: Ξ is known and holds eventually

- $\diamond$?ABC model: Ξ is unknown and holds eventually

For the latter two models, we assume that only relevant cycles starting at or after some (unknown) consistent cut $\mathcal{C}_{GST}$ (replacing the "global stabilization time" of Dwork et al. (1988)) in the execution graph satisfy (3.2).

Due to the "indistinguishability" of the ABC model and the Θ-Model for Θ-like algorithms, established in Chapter 5, one can immediately use the algorithms proposed by (Widder and Schmid, 2009) for providing eventual lock-step rounds in the ?Θ-, ◇Θ-, and ◇?Θ-Models to achieve the same in the ?ABC model, ◇ABC model, and ◇?ABC model.

In the case of the ?ABC model and the ◇?ABC model, the resulting algorithms are not particularly efficient, however, since they double the round duration with every round. A more clever algorithm could exploit the ABC synchrony condition to eventually learn a feasible value for Ξ: Suppose p's current estimate $\hat{\Xi}$ of Ξ is 2 in the execution depicted in Figure 3.4 on Page 3.4. In the computing step ψ, process p finds out that either $\hat{\Xi} = 2$ is wrong or p_{slow} has crashed; it can hence increase its estimate $\hat{\Xi}$ as soon as the slow message from p_{slow} arrives. The definition and analysis of such refined algorithms is a subject to future work.

An orthogonal way of weakening the ABC model is to drop all cycles from the space-time diagram that exceed a certain length. The clock synchronization algorithm presented in Chapter 4 will still work correctly even in an ABC model where only cycles consisting of at most 2 forward messages are considered.

It is still an open question, however, whether the ABC model can contribute another step beyond the currently weakest model by (Hutle et al., 2009) for solving consensus in the presence of crash failures. Both the time-freeness and the non-global scope of the ABC synchrony condition make it a promising candidate. However, answering this question boils down to finding "minimum" execution graphs (recall Section 3.1), i.e., ways of dropping almost all messages (and hence exempting them from the ABC synchrony condition) except for a minimal set that cannot be dropped without running into the FLP impossibility.

For example, one could just adopt the idea underlying the simple Ω failure detector (Chandra and Toueg, 1996) for the Θ-Model (Biely and Widder, 2009): The ABC synchrony condition could be restricted to a fixed subset of $f + 2$ processes in the system, which elect a leader among themselves and disseminate its id to the remaining processes in the system. By virtue of our "model indistinguishability" result (see Chapter 5), it immediately follows that the algorithms of (Biely and Widder, 2009) are correct Ω-implementation in the ABC model as well. Similarly, using a quite straightforward extension of the ABC model to time-driven systems (a process can model time-driven execution by sending messages to itself), it would also possible to adapt the Ω-implementations developed for the WTL models to the ABC model.

Chapter 4

Byzantine Clock Synchronization in the ABC Model

> Don't walk behind me; I may not lead. Don't walk in front of me; I may not follow. Just walk beside me and be my friend.
>
> *(Albert Camus)*

WE WILL SHOW in this chapter that the fault-tolerant generation algorithm introduced by Widder and Schmid (2009) can be used for clock synchronization in the ABC model.

Since processes do not have access to local hardware clocks in the ABC model, we do not consider fault-tolerant clock synchronization in the classical sense (see Lamport and Melliar-Smith, 1985). Instead, we consider *logical* clock synchronization, where every process maintains a designated clock integer variable that can be increased whenever the process takes a computing step. While this might appear to be an unnatural assumption at first sight, it makes sense from an systems point of view, since such a clock-free design has the benefit of getting by without any underlying free-running clock source, which otherwise would present a single point of failure and therefore limit the achievable level of fault-tolerance (see Fuegger et al., 2006).

CHAPTER 4. BYZANTINE CLOCK SYNCHRONIZATION

4.1. The Clock Synchronization Algorithm

Algorithm 1 Byzantine Clock Synchronization

Variables and Initialization:
1: $k \in \mathbb{N}$ initially 0;
2: send (tick 0) to all [once];

3: **if** received (tick l) from $f + 1$ distinct processes
    and $l > k$ **then**   // catch-up rule
4:    send (tick $k + 1$),...,(tick l) to all [once];
5:    $k \leftarrow l$;

6: **if** received (tick k) from $n - f$ distinct processes **then**   // advance rule
7:    send (tick $k + 1$) to all [once];
8:    $k \leftarrow k + 1$;

Algorithm 1 tolerates up to f Byzantine process failures in a system consisting of a fully connected network of
$$n \geqslant 3f + 1$$
processes adhering to the ABC model and works as follows: Every process p maintains a local variable k that constitutes p's local clock as follows: Initially, process p sets $k \leftarrow 0$ and broadcasts the message (*tick* 0); for simplicity, we assume that a process sends messages also to itself. If a correct process p receives $f + 1$ (*tick* ℓ) messages (catch-up rule, Line 3), it can be sure that at least one of them was sent by a correct process that has already reached clock value l. Therefore, p can safely catch-up to l and broadcast

$$(tick\ k+1),\ldots,(tick\ l).$$

If some process p receives

$$n - f \geqslant 2f + 1$$

(*tick k*) messages (advance rule, Line 6) and thus advances its clock to $k + 1$, it follows that at least $f + 1$ of those messages will also be received by every other correct process, which then executes Line 3. Hence, all correct processes will eventually receive $n - f$ (*tick k*) messages and advance their clock to $k + 1$.

4.1.1. Progress and Precision of Clocks

We will now prove that the algorithm guarantees progress of clocks and a certain synchrony condition, which can be stated in terms of consistent cuts in the execution graph. Note that using causality as a reference—rather than a common point in time, as in traditional clock synchronization—is natural in the time-free ABC model. Since the classic definition of consistent cuts does not take faulty processes into account, we will use the following correct-restricted version that fits to our notion of execution graphs:

Definition 4.1.1 (Consistent Cut). Let G be an execution graph and denote by $\xrightarrow{*}$ the reflexive and transitive closure of the edge relation $\rightarrow$. A subset $\mathcal{S}$ of events in G is called *consistent cut*, if

(a) for every correct process p, there is an event $\phi \in \mathcal{S}$ taking place at p, and

(b) the set $\mathcal{S}$ is left-closed for $\xrightarrow{*}$; i.e., $\mathcal{S}$ contains the whole causal past of all events in $\mathcal{S}$.

Given an event ϕ_p at process p, we denote by $C_p(\phi_p)$ the clock value *after* executing the computing step corresponding to ϕ_p. Recall that the latter need not be correctly executed if p is faulty. The clock value of a (correct) process p in the frontier of a consistent cut $\mathcal{S}$ is denoted by $C_p(\mathcal{S})$; it is the last clock value of p w.r.t. $\xrightarrow{*}$ in $\mathcal{S}$. Since it follows immediately from the code of Algorithm 1 that local clock values of correct processes are monotonically increasing, $C_p(\mathcal{S})$ is the maximum clock value at p over all events $\phi_p \in \mathcal{S}$.

We will first show that correct clocks make progress perpetually.

Lemma 4.1.2 (One step progress). *Let $\mathcal{S}$ be a consistent cut such that all correct processes p satisfy*

$$C_p(\mathcal{S}) \geq k,$$

for a fixed $k \geq 0$. Then there is a consistent cut $\mathcal{S}'$ where every correct process has set its clock to at least $k + 1$.

Proof. If all correct processes p_i have a (possibly distinct) clock value $k_i \geq k$ in the frontier of $\mathcal{S}$, the code of Algorithm 1 ensures that they have already sent (*tick k*). Since all messages in transit are eventually delivered, there must be a (not necessarily consistent) cut $\mathcal{S}''$, in the frontier of which every correct process has received $n - f$ tick k messages and thus set its clock to $k + 1$. The left-closure of $\mathcal{S}''$ yields the sought consistent cut $\mathcal{S}'$. □

Theorem 4.1.3 (*Progress*)

> In every admissible execution of Algorithm 1 in a system with $n \geqslant 3f + 1$ processes, the clock of every correct process progresses without bound.

Proof. The theorem follows from a trivial induction argument using Lemma 4.1.2, in conjunction with the fact that the cut $\mathcal{S}^0$ comprising the initial event ϕ_p^0 of every process p is trivially consistent and satisfies $C_p(\mathcal{S}^0) \geqslant 0$. □

We will now show that our logical clocks guarantee a certain kind of precision, for which we will need the following technical lemma.

Lemma 4.1.4 (First advance). *If a correct process q sets its clock to $k \geqslant 1$ in event ψ_q, then there is a correct process p that sets its clock to k using the advance rule in some event ψ_p with $\psi_p \stackrel{*}{\to} \psi_q$.*

Proof. If q uses the advance rule for setting its clock to k in ψ_q, the lemma is trivially true. If q uses the catch-up rule instead, it must have received $f + 1$ (*tick k*) messages, at least one of which was sent by a correct process q' in an event $\psi_{q'} \stackrel{*}{\to} \psi_q$. If q' also sent its (*tick k*) via the catch-up rule (Line 3), we apply the same reasoning to q'. Since every process sends (*tick k*) only once and there are only finitely many processes, we must eventually reach a correct process p that sends (*tick k*) in event $\psi_p \stackrel{*}{\to} \psi_q$ via the advance rule. □

Lemma 4.1.5 (Causal chain length). *Assume that a correct process sets its clock to $k + m$, for some $k \geqslant 0$ and $m \geqslant 0$, at some event ϕ', or has already done so. Then, there is a causal chain D of length $|D| \geqslant m$ involving correct processes only, which ends at ϕ' and starts at some event ϕ where a correct process sets its clock to k using the advance rule ($k \geqslant 1$) or the initialization rule ($k = 0$).*

Proof. Let p be the process where ϕ' occurs. If p has set its clock in some earlier computing step $\phi''' \stackrel{*}{\to} \phi'$, we just replace ϕ' by ϕ''' and continue with the case where p sets its clock to $k + m$ in ϕ'. If p sets its clock in ϕ' using the catch-up rule, applying Lemma 4.1.4 yields a correct process that sets its clock to $k+m$ in an event $\psi \stackrel{*}{\to} \phi'$ using the advance rule. To prove Lemma 4.1.5, it hence suffices to assume that p sets its clock to $k + m$ in ϕ' via the advance rule ($k + m \geqslant 1$) or the initialization rule ($k + m = 0$), as we can append the chains cut before to finally get the sought causal chain D.

The proof is by induction on m. For $m = 0$, the lemma is trivially true. For $m > 0$, at least

$$n - 2f \geqslant f + 1$$

correct processes must have sent $(tick\ k+m-1)$. Let q be any such process, and ϕ'' be the event in which $(tick\ k+m-1)$ is sent. Since q also sets its clock to $k+m-1$ at ϕ'', we can invoke Lemma 4.1.4 in case

$$k+m-1 \geqslant 1$$

to assure that the advance rule is used in ϕ''; for $k+m-1 = 0$, the initialization rule is used in ϕ''. We can hence apply the induction hypothesis and conclude that there is a causal chain D' of length at least $m-1$ leading to ϕ''. Hence, appending q's $(tick\ k+m-1)$ message [and the initially cut off chains] to D' provides D with $|D| \geqslant m$. □

The following Lemma 4.1.6 will be instrumental in our proof that Algorithm 1 maintains synchronized clocks. It reveals that when a correct process p updates its clock value in some event ϕ', then all messages of correct processes of a certain lower tick value must have already been received by p, i.e., must originate from the causal cone of ϕ'.

Lemma 4.1.6 (Causal Cone). *For some $k \geqslant 0$, suppose that*

$$C_p(\phi') = k + 2\Xi$$

at the event ϕ' of a correct process p. Then, for every $0 \leqslant \ell \leqslant k$, process p has already received $(tick\ \ell)$ from every correct process.

Proof. The general proof idea is to show that the arrival of $(tick\ \ell)$ in some event ϕ'' after ϕ' would close a relevant cycle in which the synchrony assumption (3.2) is violated. See Figure 4.1 for a graphical representation of the scenario described below.

Let $C_p(\phi') = k+2\Xi$ and assume, for the sake of contradiction, that $(tick\ \ell)$ from some correct process q was not yet received by p before or at ϕ', for some $\ell \leqslant k$. Consider the last message that p received from q before (or at) ϕ'. If such a message exists, we denote its send event at q as ψ'; otherwise, we simply define ψ' to be the (externally triggered) initial computing step at q.

From Lemma 4.1.5, we know that there is a causal chain

$$D = \phi'_1 \to \cdots \to \phi'$$

of length

$$|D| \geqslant k + 2\Xi - (\ell+1),$$

where a (*tick* $\ell+1$) message is sent in ϕ_1' by some correct process p_1 via the advance rule and, by assumption, $C_p(\phi') = k + 2\Xi$. Since ϕ_1' executes the advance rule, p_1 must have received $n - f$ (*tick* ℓ) messages to do so. Denoting by $0 \leqslant f' \leqslant f$ the actual number of faulty processes, it follows that

$$n - f - f' \geqslant f + 1$$

of these messages were sent by correct processes; we denote this set by P_1.

Since Theorem 4.1.3 ensures progress of all correct processes, there must be an event ψ_1, coinciding with or occurring after ψ', in which q broadcasts (*tick* ℓ). Eventually, this message is received by p in some event ϕ'', which must be after ϕ' since by assumption (*tick* ℓ) was not received before (or at) ϕ'. Furthermore, we claim that q receives at least $n - f' - f$ (*tick* ℓ) messages from correct processes after (or at) event ψ_1; let P_2 be that set. Otherwise, q would have received at least

$$n - f' - (n - f' - f) + 1 = f + 1$$

(*tick* ℓ) messages from correct processes by some event

$$\psi_1' \xrightarrow{*} \psi_1,$$

and therefore would have broadcast (*tick* ℓ) already in ψ_1' according to the catch-up rule.

Since $P_1 \cup P_2$ is of size at most $2n - 2f' - 2f$ and we have only $n - f'$ correct processes, it follows by the pigeonhole principle that

$$2n - 2f' - 2f - (n - f') = n - 2f - f' \geqslant n - 3f > 0$$

correct processes are in $P_1 \cap P_2$. Choose any process

$$p_0 \in P_1 \cap P_2,$$

which broadcasts its (*tick* ℓ) in some event ϕ_0. This message is received at q in some event ψ_2, and at p_1 in event ϕ_1.

It is immediately apparent from Figure 4.1 that the causal chains

$$\phi_0 \to \phi_1 \xrightarrow{*} D \xrightarrow{*} \phi'',\ \phi_0 \to \psi_2,\ \psi_1 \xrightarrow{*} \psi_2,\ \text{and } \psi_1 \to \phi''$$

form a relevant cycle Z: The number of backward messages is

$$|Z^-| = |D| + 1 \geqslant k - \ell + 2\Xi \geqslant 2\Xi,$$

since $\ell \leqslant k$; the number of forward messages $|Z^+|$ is 2. But this yields

$$\frac{|Z^-|}{|Z^+|} \geqslant \frac{2\Xi}{2} = \Xi,$$

contradicting the ABC synchrony assumption (3.2). □

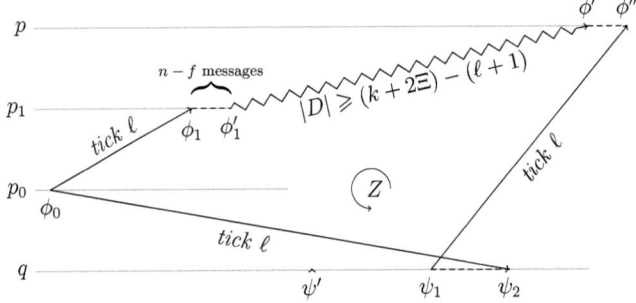

Figure 4.1.: Proof of Lemma 4.1.6

We can now easily prove that Algorithm 1 maintains the following synchrony condition:

Theorem 4.1.7 (*Synchrony*)

For any consistent cut $\mathcal{S}$ in an admissible execution of Algorithm 1 in a system with $n \geqslant 3f + 1$ processes, we have

$$|C_p(\mathcal{S}) - C_q(\mathcal{S})| \leqslant 2\Xi$$

for all correct processes p and q.

Proof. Assume that the maximum clock value in the frontier of $\mathcal{S}$ is $k + 2\Xi$, and let p be a correct process with

$$C_p(\mathcal{S}) = k + 2\Xi.$$

From Lemma 4.1.6, we know that p must have seen (*tick* ℓ) from every correct process q for any $\ell \leqslant k$. Since $\mathcal{S}$ is consistent, all the corresponding send events at q must be within $\mathcal{S}$, such that $C_q(\mathcal{S}) \geqslant k$. □

Even though the ABC model is entirely time-free, we can immediately transfer the above synchrony property to real-time cuts according to the results of Mattern (1992), in order to derive the following theorem:

Theorem 4.1.8 (*Clock Precision*)

Let $C_p(t)$ denote the clock value of process p at real-time t. For any time t of an admissible execution of Algorithm 1 in a system with $n \geqslant 3f + 1$ processes, we have

$$|C_p(t) - C_q(t)| \leqslant 2\Xi,$$

for all correct processes p and q.

4.1.2. Clock Synchronization with Bounded Progress

We have already seen that in Algorithm 1 clocks make progress perpetually and remain synchronized while doing so. However, *precision* and *progress* define a fairly weak version of the clock synchronization problem only. In our setting, for example, one could easily simulate optimal precision clock synchronization (i.e., a precision of 1) by introducing an artificial "macro"-clock, which ticks once every 2Ξ ticks of our "micro"-clock C_p.[1] Optimal precision of the "macro"-clocks would also be maintained if we increased X with every "macro"-clock tick throughout the execution.[2] Clearly, X would grow without bound in such a simulation, which makes it apparent that neither precision nor progress constrains the rate of progress (w.r.t. logical time) of a clock synchronization algorithm.

In classic clock synchronization, this is usually enforced by means of some *linear envelope condition*, which asserts a linear relation between clock time and real-time and thereby also rules out "degenerated" solutions (Dolev et al., 1986). In our asynchronous setting, we obviously cannot refer to real-time, but what we can do is to relate the rate of progress of the fastest and the slowest correct clock to each other. We will show that our algorithm also satisfies a suitably defined *bounded progress condition* based on consistent cuts as defined in Definition 4.1.10 below.

---

[1] In fact, this is the main idea of the lock-step round simulation Algorithm 2 below.
[2] This can be used to simulate eventual lock-step rounds in the weaker variants of the ABC model introduced in Section 3.5, cp. Widder and Schmid (2009).

Definition 4.1.9 (Consistent Cut Interval). Let ϕ be an event at a correct process and denote the left closure w.r.t. the causality relation $\to$ as $\langle\phi\rangle$. If ψ is an event such that $\phi \to \psi$, we define the *consistent cut interval* as

$$[\langle\phi\rangle, \langle\psi\rangle] := \langle\psi\rangle \setminus \langle\phi\rangle.$$

Note that, when considering the real-time transformation of Mattern (1992), a consistent cut interval can essentially be seen as a real-time interval. Since the ABC model is a message-driven model, we only care about the rate of progress of certain *distinguished events* that affect the message complexity, i.e., we do not want to include events where messages are only received but not sent.

Definition 4.1.10 (Bounded Progress Condition). An algorithm A has *bounded progress* ϱ for some (set of) distinguished events *iff* the following holds true in all admissible executions of A: Whenever a correct process p performs at least $\varrho > 0$ distinguished events in a consistent cut interval $[\langle\phi_p\rangle, \langle\phi'_p\rangle]$, every correct process performs at least one distinguished event in $[\langle\phi_p\rangle, \langle\phi'_p\rangle]$.

Theorem 4.1.11

> Algorithm 1 has the bounded progress
>
> $$\varrho = 4\Xi + 1$$
>
> for the distinguished event that represents clock incrementing and message broadcasting, i.e., send to all.

Proof. From the code of Algorithm 1, it is apparent that incrementing the clock value and broadcasting messages is done in the same step. Let the distinguished events considered here be exactly those steps. Suppose that a correct process p has performed at least $4\Xi + 1$ distinguished events in between events ϕ_p and ϕ'_p, i.e., in the cut interval $[\langle\phi_p\rangle, \langle\phi'_p\rangle]$. Furthermore, assume in contradiction that there is a correct process q that does not perform any distinguished event in $[\langle\phi_p\rangle, \langle\phi'_p\rangle]$. Assuming that

$$C_p(\langle\phi_p\rangle) = k,$$

for some $k \geqslant 0$, it follows that

$$C_p(\langle\phi'_p\rangle) \geqslant k + 4\Xi + 1.$$

By assumption, q does not perform a distinguished event in $[\langle\phi_p\rangle, \langle\phi'_p\rangle]$, hence

$$C_q(\langle\phi_p\rangle) = C_q(\langle\phi'_p\rangle).$$

We distinguish two cases for the number of distinguished events, i.e., the clock values, in event ϕ_p:

1. $C_p(\langle\phi_p\rangle) > C_q(\langle\phi_p\rangle)$: Since $C_q(\langle\phi_p\rangle) = C_q(\langle\phi'_p\rangle)$, we immediately arrive at a contradiction to Theorem 4.1.7.

2. $C_p(\langle\phi_p\rangle) \leqslant C_q(\langle\phi_p\rangle)$: We have

$$C_p(\langle\phi'_p\rangle) - C_q(\langle\phi'_p\rangle) \geqslant k + 4\Xi + 1 - C_q(\langle\phi'_p\rangle) = C_p(\langle\phi_p\rangle) - C_q(\langle\phi'_p\rangle) + 4\Xi + 1$$
$$\geqslant C_p(\langle\phi_p\rangle) - C_q(\langle\phi_p\rangle) + 4\Xi + 1.$$

Applying Theorem 4.1.7 to $C_p(\langle\phi_p\rangle) - C_q(\langle\phi_p\rangle)$ yields

$$C_p(\langle\phi'_p\rangle) - C_q(\langle\phi'_p\rangle) \geqslant -2\Xi + 4\Xi + 1 = 2\Xi + 1,$$

contradicting Theorem 4.1.7 for $\langle\phi'_p\rangle$.

$\square$

From the general perspective of solvability, Theorem 4.1.11 shows that "bounded" clock synchronization is solvable in the ABC model. The following corollary makes this fact explicit and puts the results of this section into the high-level perspective of Figure 1.2 on Page 21.

Corollary 4.1.12. *Bounded clock synchronization is solvable in the ABC model.*

4.2. Simulating Lock-Step Rounds

Finally, we will show how to build a lock-step round simulation in the ABC model atop of Algorithm 1. A lock-step round execution proceeds in a sequence of rounds $r = 1, 2, \ldots$, where all correct processes take their round r computing steps (consisting of receiving the round $r-1$ messages[3], executing a state transition, and broadcasting the round r messages for the next round) exactly at the same time.

---
[3] For notational convenience, we enumerate the messages with the index of the previous round.

Algorithm 2 A Lock-Step Round Simulation Tolerating Byzantine Faults

Variables and Initialization:
1: $r \in \mathbb{N}$ initially 0;
2: call start(0);

3: Whenever k is updated do
4:   **if** $k/(2\Xi) = r + 1$ **then**
5:     $r \leftarrow r + 1$
6:     call start(r)

7: **procedure** start(r:integer)
8:   **if** $r > 0$ **then**
9:     read round $r - 1$ messages
10:     execute round r computation
11:     send round r messages

We use the same simulation as Widder and Schmid (2009), which just considers clocks as phase counters and introduces rounds consisting of 2Ξ phases. Algorithm 2 shows the code that must be merged with Algorithm 1; the round r messages are piggybacked on (*tick k*) messages every 2Ξ phases, namely, when $k/(2\Xi) = r$. The round r computing step[4] is encapsulated in the function start(r) in Line 7; start(0) just sends the round 0 messages that will be processed in the round 1 computing step.

To prove that this algorithm achieves lock-step rounds, we need to show that all round r messages from correct processes have arrived at every correct process p before p enters round $r + 1$, i.e., executes start($r + 1$).

Theorem 4.2.1 (*Lock-Step Rounds*)
> In a system with
> $$n \geqslant 3f + 1$$
> processes, Algorithm 2 merged with Algorithm 1 correctly simulates lock-step rounds in the ABC model.

Proof. Suppose that a correct process p starts round $r + 1$ in event ϕ. By the code, $C_p(\phi) = k$ with
$$k/(2\Xi) = r + 1, \text{ i.e., } k = 2\Xi r + 2\Xi.$$

---
[4]Note that we assume that computing steps happen atomically in zero time.

By way of contradiction, assume that the round r message, sent by some correct process q in the event ψ, arrives at p only after ϕ. By the code,

$$C_q(\psi) = k' \text{ with } k'/(2\Xi) = r, \text{ i.e., } k' = 2\Xi r.$$

However, Lemma 4.1.6 reveals that p should have already seen ($tick$ $2\Xi r$) from q before event ϕ, a contradiction. □

4.3. Discussion

In this chapter we have shown that the causality based synchrony condition of the ABC model is sufficient for achieving synchrony despite Byzantine processes.

Actually, the proofs in this chapter establish *uniform* (see Hadzilacos and Toueg, 1993) lock-step rounds, i.e., lock-step rounds that are also obeyed by faulty processes until they behave erroneously for the first time: If the messages sent by faulty processes also obey the ABC synchrony condition (3.2), then the proof of the key Lemma 4.1.6 actually establishes a uniform causal cone property: Assuming that

(i) process q performs correctly up to and including at least one more step after event ψ', and

(ii) p works correctly up to and including event ϕ',

then p would receive (though not necessarily process) the message from q in ϕ'', thereby closing a relevant cycle that violates Ξ. Hence, p must have received all messages from its causal cone by ϕ' already, which carries over to a uniform version of Theorem 4.2.1.

One (strong) assumption that we have made throughout this chapter is that underlying communication network is fully connected. Due to the recent rise in popularity of dynamic networks (see for example Kuhn et al., 2010), an interesting direction of our future research is concerned with weakening the connectivity assumption. It is possible to extend our algorithms to *sparse network* scenarios: Assuming only crash failures, it is sufficient if the network graph is at least $(f+1)$-connected. Handling Byzantine processes, however, requires a stronger restriction on the network topology.

Chapter 5

Indistinguishability of the ABC Model and the Θ-Model

> We are always more anxious to be distinguished for a talent which we do not possess, than to be praised for the fifteen which we do possess.
>
> (Mark Twain)

THE INDISTINGUISHABILITY OF SYSTEM MODELS is a frequently used argument for showing that the properties of a specific algorithm that were proven to hold in one model also hold in another model. For example, the following is a (rather trivial) model indistinguishability argument that is often used in conjunction with asynchronous algorithms, which obviously work correctly also in synchronous systems: Since synchronous admissible runs are just a subset of the runs admissible in $\mathcal{M}^{ASYNC}$, every property guaranteed by an algorithm in the asynchronous model also holds in the synchronous model.

In this chapter, we will develop a non-trivial model indistinguishability argument which enables us to show that any algorithm designed for the Θ-Model (Le Lann and Schmid, 2003; Widder et al., 2005; Widder and Schmid, 2009) also works correctly in our ABC model, presented in Chapter 3.

It is non-trivial, since most of the admissible ABC executions are *not* admissible in the Θ-Model. Nevertheless, no additional simulation layer will be involved in our argument:

the original Θ-algorithms can be used "as is" in the ABC model, without sacrificing performance!

More specifically, provided that $\Xi < \Theta$, where Θ is the system parameter of the Θ-Model defined below, we will show that every algorithm designed and proved correct for the Θ-Model will also "work" (w.r.t. timing independent properties) in the corresponding ABC model with parameter Ξ. Since the algorithms analyzed in Section 4 are essentially the same as the algorithms for clock synchronization and lock-step round simulation in the Θ-Model introduced in (Widder and Schmid, 2009), one may wonder whether it would not have been possible to just transfer the results of the Θ-based analysis to the ABC model using these results. This is not possible, however, since some of the properties studied in (Widder and Schmid, 2009) refer to real-time and are hence not timing independent.

5.1. The Θ-Model

Just like the ABC model, all variants of the Θ-Model are message-driven models, i.e., every computing step is triggered by exactly one incoming message, and processes can communicate by broadcasting messages. It is essential that the ABC model and the Θ-Model have compatible system assumptions in order to ensure that every algorithm A of one model can be run in the other without non-trivial adaptations. The only significant difference concerns synchrony assumptions, which we will discuss next:

Definition 5.1.1. In the simple *static Θ-Model* (Le Lann and Schmid, 2003), it is assumed that there are (unknown but finite) upper resp. lower bounds $\tau^+ > 0$ resp. $0 < \tau^- \leqslant \tau^+$ on the end-to-end delays of all correct messages in all admissible runs. The ratio of τ^+ to τ^- matches the model parameter

$$\Theta = \frac{\tau^+}{\tau^-}. \qquad (5.1)$$

As the static Θ-Model does not sufficiently capture the case where end-to-end delays grow without bound throughout a run, Widder and Schmid (2009) introduced a more flexible version of condition (5.1): Let $\tau^+(t)$ respectively $\tau^-(t)$ denote the maximum resp. minimum end-to-end delay of all messages in transit at time t.

Definition 5.1.2. A run is admissible in the *dynamic Θ-Model*, if

$$\forall t: \frac{\tau^+(t)}{\tau^-(t)} \leqslant \Theta,$$

for some fixed system parameter Θ.

Clearly, the synchrony assumption of the dynamic model variant is more relaxed, in the sense that $\tau^+(t)$ and $\tau^-(t)$ are a function of real-time.[1] That is, the ratio between upper and lower bound of the end-to-end delay of messages that are in transit simultaneously, is bounded by Θ at all times.

However, for the purpose of this chapter, it is sufficient to consider only the simpler static Θ-model, as these two variants been shown to be equivalent from the point of view of solvability power (see Widder and Schmid, 2009).

5.2. System Properties as Sets of Runs

In this section we will formalize the meaning of "solving a specific problem", which we have already informally introduced in Section 1.1. Consider the runs of some fixed algorithm A. Let $\mathcal{M}^{\text{ASYNC}}$ be the set of runs of A that are admissible in the asynchronous system model. Note that we consider *timed runs* here, i.e., runs along with the occurrence times of their events, as measured by the discrete clock T (see Chapter 2).

Definition 5.2.1. A *property* P is a subset of the runs generated by some algorithm A in $\mathcal{M}^{\text{ASYNC}}$.

In other words, a property is defined by the runs of A that satisfy it. Let $\mathcal{M}$ be the set of admissible runs of A in some model M that restricts the asynchronous model, by adding additional constraints like for example the ABC synchrony condition (3.2). Clearly, $\mathcal{M}$ is the intersection of some model-specific safety and liveness properties in $\mathcal{M}^{\text{ASYNC}}$, since it was shown by Alpern and Schneider (1985) that every property can be expressed as the intersection of some safety and liveness properties.

Definition 5.2.2. We say that an execution (or run) α *is in model M* if $\alpha \in \mathcal{M}$, i.e., if α is admissible in M. If $\mathcal{M} \subseteq P$, we say that algorithm A *satisfies* property P in the model M.

Since there is no notion of real-time in the ABC model, we restrict the focus of this chapter to so called timing independent properties.

---
[1] Note that t refers to real time in the Θ-Model.

Definition 5.2.3 (Timing independent property). A property P is called *timing independent*, if

$$\alpha \in P \Rightarrow \alpha' \in P,$$

for every pair of causally equivalent executions α, α', i.e., executions where $G_\alpha = G_{\alpha'}$.

Using a trivial model-indistinguishability argument, it is easy to show that properties of an algorithm proved to hold in the ABC model also hold in the Θ-Model, for any $\Theta < \Xi$: The following Theorem 5.2.4 exploits the fact that the relevant cycles in the execution graph G_α, corresponding to an admissible execution α in the Θ-Model, also satisfy the ABC synchrony condition (3.2), i.e., α is an admissible execution in the ABC model as well. We denote the set of executions that are admissible in the Θ-Model (resp. ABC model) as $\mathcal{M}^\Theta$ (resp. $\mathcal{M}^{ABC}$).

Theorem 5.2.4

> For any $\Theta < \Xi$, it holds that $\mathcal{M}^\Theta \subseteq \mathcal{M}^{ABC}$. Hence, if an algorithm satisfies a property P in the ABC model, it also satisfies P in the Θ-Model.

Proof. If Z is any relevant cycle in G_α, then no more than $|Z^+|\Theta$ backward messages can be in Z; otherwise, at least one forward-backward message pair would violate (5.1). It follows that $|Z^-|/|Z^+| \leqslant \Theta < \Xi$ as required. Hence, $\mathcal{M}^\Theta \subseteq \mathcal{M}^{ABC} \subseteq P$, since the algorithm satisfies P in the ABC model. $\square$

The converse of Theorem 5.2.4 is not true, however: The time-free synchrony assumption (3.2) of the ABC model allows arbitrary small end-to-end delays for individual messages, violating (5.1) for every Θ. For example, see Figure 3.1 on Page 31, where the end-to-end delays of messages m_1 and m_6 would require a very large Θ to be admissible in the Θ-Model. Given any fixed Θ, we could easily violate (5.1) by letting the delay of message m_1 converge to 0. Therefore, from the perspective of model coverage, the ABC model is indeed strictly weaker than the Θ-Model, hence $\mathcal{M}^{ABC} \not\subseteq \mathcal{M}^\Theta$. Nevertheless, Theorem 5.3.1 below shows that, given an arbitrary finite execution graph G in $\mathcal{M}^{ABC}$, it is always possible to assign end-to-end delays in $(1, \Xi)$ to the individual messages *without changing the event order* at any process.

5.3. Indistinguishability for Timing Independent Properties

We will now show that any timing independent property that holds in the Θ-Model, also holds in the ABC model. For safety properties, it will turn out that we can "deform" the execution graph (see Chapter 3) of a given run in the ABC model generated by some algorithm A (that was originally designed for the Θ-Model) in a way that does not change the event ordering but satisfies (5.1).

Theorem 5.3.1

> Let G be the (finite) execution graph of some prefix of a run in the ABC model. There is an end-to-end delay assignment function τ, such that the weighted execution graph G^τ is causally equivalent to G and all messages in G^τ satisfy (5.1).

Since we first want to present the main indistinguishability argument from a more high level perspective, we delay the very involved proof of Theorem 5.3.1 until Section 5.4.

For now, we will assume that Theorem 5.3.1 is true and informally argue why our indistinguishability result holds: Let τ be such a delay assignment function, and let G^τ be the weighted execution graph obtained from G by assigning the corresponding delays to the messages. Since Θ-algorithms are message-driven and do not have access to hardware clocks, G and G^τ are indistinguishable for every process, as the sequence of events and state transitions is exactly the same. Consequently, an algorithm that provides certain timing independent properties when being run in the Θ-Model also maintains these properties in the ABC model, as stated in the main result, Theorem 5.3.7, below.

5.3.1. Safety Properties

In order to formally prove the claimed model indistinguishability of the ABC model and the Θ-Model, we proceed with the following Lemma 5.3.2. It says that processes cannot notice any difference in finite prefixes in the ABC model and in the Θ-Model, and therefore make the same state transitions.

Lemma 5.3.2 (Safety equivalence). *If an algorithm satisfies a timing independent safety property S in the Θ-Model, then S also holds in the ABC model, for any $\Xi < \Theta$.*

Proof. Suppose, by way of contradiction, that there is a finite prefix β of an ABC model execution $\alpha \in \mathcal{M}^{\text{ABC}}$, where S does not hold. Furthermore, let β' be a finite extension of β such that all messages sent by correct processes in β arrive in β', and denote the execution graph of β' by $G_{\beta'}$. From Theorem 5.3.1, we know that there is a delay assignment τ such that the synchrony assumption (5.1) of the Θ-Model is satisfied for all messages in the timed execution graph $G_{\beta'}^\tau$, while the causality relation in $G_{\beta'}$ and $G_{\beta'}^\tau$ (and, since $G_{\beta'}^\tau \supseteq G_\beta^\tau$, also in G_β and G_β^τ) is the same.

We will now construct an admissible execution γ in the Θ-Model, which has the same prefix $G_{\beta'}^\tau$: If t is the latest occurrence time of all events in $G_{\beta'}^\tau$, we simply assign an end-to-end delay of τ^+ to all messages still in transit at time t and to all messages sent at a later point in time. Note that γ may be totally different from the ABC-execution α with respect to the event ordering *after* the common prefix β'. However, due to this τ^+-assignment, γ is admissible in the Θ-Model since (5.1) holds for all messages, but violates S, which provides the required contradiction. □

5.3.2. The Topology on Runs

Unfortunately, we cannot use the above reasoning for transferring liveness properties from the Θ-Model to the ABC model, since the indistinguishability of finite prefixes of an execution is not sufficient to show that "something good" must eventually happen or happens infinitely often. Nevertheless, Theorem 5.3.5 below will reveal that all properties satisfiable by an algorithm in the Θ-Model can be reduced to (possibly stronger) safety properties, in the following sense: For every property P (which could be a liveness property like eventual termination) satisfied by A in $\mathcal{M}_\Theta$, there is actually a (typically stronger) safety property $P' \subseteq P$ (like termination within time X) that is also satisfied by A in $\mathcal{M}_\Theta$ and immediately implies P. Hence, there is no need to deal with liveness properties here at all!

For our proof, we utilize the convenient topological framework introduced by Alpern and Schneider (1985), where safety properties correspond to closed sets of executions in $\mathcal{M}^{\text{ASYNC}}$, and liveness properties correspond to dense sets:

Definition 5.3.3. Let α and β be infinite runs in some model M. The function $d : \mathcal{M} \times \mathcal{M} \to \mathbb{R}$ defined as

$$d(\alpha, \beta) = \begin{cases} 0 & \alpha \text{ and } \beta \text{ are the same;} \\ 2^{-N} & \alpha \text{ and } \beta \text{ are distinct,} \end{cases}$$

where N is the index of the first event where α and β differ.

It can easily be shown that d is a metric and therefore induces a metric space on the set of runs $\mathcal{M}$. This topological space has the so called ε-balls as basic open sets, defined as

$$B_\varepsilon(\alpha) = \{\beta \in \mathcal{M} \mid d(\alpha, \beta) < \varepsilon\}. \tag{5.2}$$

We will now show that safety properties correspond to closed sets: If an execution α does not satisfy a safety property P_s, i.e. $\alpha \notin P_s$, then there is an index N where all executions β that share a prefix longer than N with α are not in P_s.[2] Formally speaking, suppose that $\alpha \notin P_s$. If there exists an $N \geq 0$ such that for all $\beta \in \mathcal{M}$ where

$$d(\alpha, \beta) < 2^{-N},$$

it follows that $\beta \notin P_s$. Thus, the set of runs P_s is *closed* by definition, since its complement is open.

If P_l is a liveness property then, for all executions α and for every $N \geq 0$, there is an execution $\beta \in P_l$ such that $d(\alpha, \beta) < \frac{1}{2^N}$. That is, no matter what a finite prefix looks like, it is always "live" in the sense that we can extend it appropriately such that liveness holds. Clearly P_l is a *dense set*, since it intersects every basic open set $B_\varepsilon(\alpha)$ defined in (5.2).

Definition 5.3.4 (Closed Model). If a model M is determined solely by safety properties $S_1, \ldots, S_k$, then the set

$$\mathcal{M} = \bigcap_{i=1}^{k} S_i$$

corresponding to the executions admissible in M is closed, since finite intersections of closed sets are closed. We say that M is a *closed model*.

Theorem 5.3.5 (*Safety-only in closed models*)

Let M be a closed model augmenting the asynchronous model, and let $\mathcal{M} \subseteq \mathcal{M}^{\text{ASYNC}}$ be the set of all admissible executions of an algorithm A in M. To show that A satisfies some arbitrary property P in M, it suffices to show that A satisfies the safety property $P' = P \cap \mathcal{M}$.

Proof. Suppose that A satisfies some property $P \subseteq \mathcal{M}^{\text{ASYNC}}$ in M, i.e., $\mathcal{M} \subseteq P$. Then, $\mathcal{M} = \mathcal{M} \cap P$ and since $\mathcal{M}$ is closed, it follows that $P' = \mathcal{M} \cap P$ is closed (in $\mathcal{M}^{\text{ASYNC}}$)

---

[2]This closely matches intuition, since once a safety property is violated in a prefix, it makes no difference how this prefix is extended.

as well. But this is exactly the definition of a safety property $P' \subseteq \mathcal{M}^{\text{ASYNC}}$ and, since $\mathcal{M} \subseteq P' \subseteq P$, it indeed suffices to show that A satisfies P' in M. □

Theorem 5.3.5 is not limited to the context of the Θ-Model, but rather applies to *any* system model that is specified by safety properties. Note carefully that this argument does not work for models that have system assumptions which must hold only *eventually*.

Lemma 5.3.6 (Closedness of Θ-Model). *The Θ-Model is closed.*

Proof. We need to show that the set $\mathcal{M}_\Theta$ of executions in the Θ-Model is closed. If some execution α violated the end-to-end timing assumption (5.1) of the Θ-Model, there would be a finite prefix of α within which this violation has happened. This characterizes a safety property in $\mathcal{M}^{\text{ASYNC}}$, which by definition coincides with some closed set. □

Theorem 5.3.5 in conjunction with Lemma 5.3.6 reveals that every property satisfiable in the Θ-Model is a safety property. Hence, Lemma 5.3.2 finally implies Theorem 5.3.7:

Theorem 5.3.7

All timing independent properties satisfied by an algorithm in the Θ-Model also hold in the ABC model, for any $\Xi < \Theta$.

5.4. Proof of Theorem 5.3.1

In this section we present the previously deferred and technically involved proof of Theorem 5.3.1, which provides the last missing piece for our indistinguishability argument.

We start our detailed treatment with the definition of a non-negative weight function τ on the edges of a given execution graph G, where τ will be such that (5.1) is satisfied for all messages in G.

5.4.1. Modeling Causality as a System of Linear Inequalities

A necessary and sufficient condition on τ for preserving the causality relation $\to$ is to require that the sum over all edges in a cycle, taking into account their direction, is zero. Recall from Chapter 3 that the edge relation of an execution graph is defined on the set of events Φ. We will now define an orientation assignment on edges.

Definition 5.4.1. Let Z be a (relevant or non-relevant) cycle (see Definition 3.1.3 on Page 31) and let the map
$$\text{sgn}_Z \colon \Phi \times \Phi \to \{-1, 0, 1\}$$
be such that
$$\text{sgn}_Z(e) = \begin{cases} +1 & \text{for } e \in \bar{Z}^-; \\ -1 & \text{for } e \in \bar{Z}^+; \\ 0 & \text{for every } e \text{ not in } Z. \end{cases}$$

Definition 5.4.2. The mapping $\tau \colon \Phi \times \Phi \to \mathbb{Q}^+$ is said to be an *assignment for the cycle Z* if
$$\sum_{e \in Z} \text{sgn}_Z(e) \tau(e) = 0. \tag{5.3}$$

Note carefully that this "zero-sum" condition must hold for all cycles. A message e that is not contained in any cycle can safely be disregarded, since any value $\tau(e)$ will do for preserving $\to$.

Definition 5.4.3. We call τ a *normalized assignment for G* if
$$1 < \tau(e) < \Xi, \tag{5.4}$$
$$0 < \tau(\bar{e}) < \infty, \tag{5.5}$$
for all non-local edges (i.e., messages) e and all local edges $\bar{e}$ in G. Furthermore, we call G together with a normalized assignment τ a *timed execution graph*, denoted as G^τ.

Due to (5.4), a normalized assignment τ satisfies (5.1) for all messages in G since $\Xi < \Theta$. In addition, condition (5.5) ensures that all receive events at the same process are strictly ordered; since $\tau(\bar{e})$ may be chosen arbitrarily small, this is not a restriction in practice. In fact, allowing $\tau(\bar{e}) = 0$ would allow a local edge $\bar{e} = (\phi_1, \phi_2)$ to "disappear", which could alter the causality relation: The event order of simultaneous receive events ϕ_1, ϕ_2 could be determined by some tie-breaking rule, which might end up with $\phi_2 \to \phi_1$.

To show the existence of a normalized assignment, for a given *finite* execution graph (corresponding to a finite prefix of an ABC execution; this is sufficient for our purposes, as we have argued in Lemma 5.3.2), we combine the above conditions on τ in a system of linear inequalities of the form $\mathbf{Ax} < \mathbf{b}$ as follows: First, we split (5.4) into the conjunction of the lower bound condition $-\tau(e) < -1$ and the upper bound condition

$\tau(e) < \Xi$, for all messages e. Moreover, assigning weights to all messages in a relevant cycle Z in a way such that

$$\sum_{e^-\in Z^-} \tau(e^-) - \sum_{e^+\in Z^+} \tau(e^+) < 0 \qquad (5.6)$$

holds, leaves "space" for assigning a positive weight to the local edges of Z, cp. Figure 3.1, and hence to satisfy (5.5). Since every cycle has at least one local edge, the local edge weights can in fact be chosen such that the required cycle condition

$$\sum_{e\in Z} \mathrm{sgn}_Z(e)\tau(e) = 0$$

also holds. The same reasoning applies if Z is a non-relevant cycle, except that the sums in (5.6) must have the opposite sign, see Figure 3.5. As a consequence, it suffices to deal with assignments τ for messages only.

Listing these conditions for, say, k messages, l relevant cycles, and m non-relevant cycles in G yields the system of linear inequalities

$$\mathbf{Ax} < \mathbf{b},$$

as illustrated in Figure 5.1. The matrix $\mathbf{A}$ is of size $n \times k$, for

$$n = 2k + l + m.$$

The coefficient x_j of the solution vector $\mathbf{x}$ is just the assignment $\tau(e_j)$ for message $e_j \in G$. The matrix-vector multiplication of the first k rows of $\mathbf{A}$ by vector $\mathbf{x}$ corresponds to the lower-bound condition on τ for each message, while the upper-bound conditions are represented by the multiplication of rows $k+1$ to $2k$ by $\mathbf{x}$. The next l rows of $\mathbf{A}$ reflect condition (5.6) for all relevant cycles Z_i; a forward message will have a coefficient -1 here, whereas a backward message has $+1$, i.e.,

$$a_{2k+i,j} = \mathrm{sgn}_{Z_i}(e_j).$$

The remaining m rows represent the sign-flipped version of (5.6) for the non-relevant cycles Z_i that is,

$$a_{2k+i,j} = -\mathrm{sgn}_{Z_i}(e_j).$$

CHAPTER 5. MODEL INDISTINGUISHABILITY

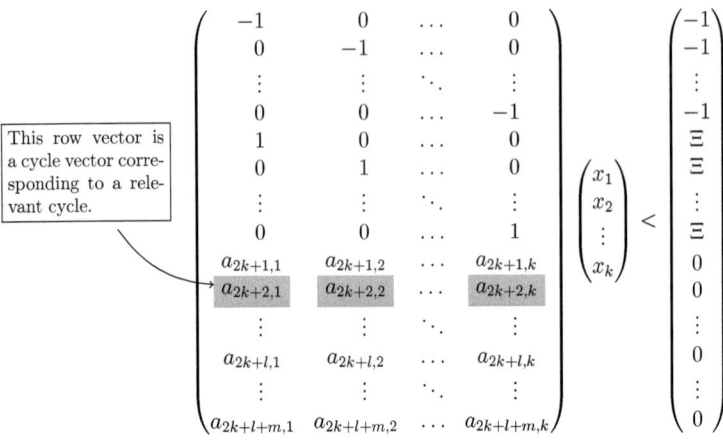

Figure 5.1.: Matrix Form of the Linear System $\mathbf{Ax} < \mathbf{b}$.

Note that $a_{2k+i,j} = 0$ for every message e_j that is not in Z_i. Figure 5.2 shows an example of this correspondence of cycles and cycle vectors.

We will use the following variant of Farkas' lemma for linear inequalities to prove that $\mathbf{Ax} < \mathbf{b}$ always has a solution, that is, a normalized assignment for G always exists.[3]

Theorem 5.4.4 (*Variant of the Farkas lemma, see Carver (1921)*)

The system $\mathbf{Ax} < \mathbf{b}$ has a solution $\mathbf{x}$ if and only if all vectors $\mathbf{y} > 0$ where $\mathbf{y}^T \mathbf{A} = 0$ satisfy $\mathbf{y}^T \mathbf{b} > 0$.

If a vector $\mathbf{y} > 0$ satisfies $\mathbf{y}^T \mathbf{A} = 0$, we have

$$\sum_{i=1}^{k} a_{i,j} y_i + \sum_{i=k+1}^{2k} a_{i,j} y_i + \sum_{i=1}^{l+m} a_{2k+i,j} y_{2k+i} = 0,$$

for all columns j in the matrix $\mathbf{A}$. Observing that the first $2k$ rows of $\mathbf{A}$ correspond to the identity matrices $-\mathbf{I}_k$ and $\mathbf{I}_k$, we can rewrite this as

$$y_{k+j} - y_j + \sum_{i=1}^{l+m} a_{2k+i,j} y_{2k+i} = 0. \tag{5.7}$$

---
[3]Note that $\mathbf{y}^T$ denotes the transpose of vector $\mathbf{y}$.

Note that we call the first $2k$ rows of $\mathbf{A}$ the *upper-part of* $\mathbf{A}$, and the first $2k$ coefficients of $\mathbf{y}$ *upper-coefficients of* $\mathbf{y}$; the rest of the rows of $\mathbf{A}$ resp. the coefficients of $\mathbf{y}$ is called *cycle-part of* $\mathbf{A}$ resp. *cycle-coefficients of* $\mathbf{y}$. Moreover, we call a row vector in the cycle-part of $\mathbf{A}$ *cycle vector*. We split the indices of the cycle-part of $\mathbf{A}$ into the set R, containing all indices $1 \leqslant i \leqslant l$ of relevant cycle vectors, and the set N, containing all indices

$$l+1 \leqslant i \leqslant l+m$$

of non-relevant cycle vectors. Since equation (5.7) sums up to zero for every column j, the sum over all columns is also zero, that is,

$$\sum_{j=1}^{k} y_{k+j} - \sum_{j=1}^{k} y_j + \sum_{i \in R \cup N} \sum_{j=1}^{k} a_{2k+i,j} y_{2k+i} = 0.$$

For a relevant cycle Z_i, the sum of the positive resp. the sum of the negative entries in a row i in the cycle-part of $\mathbf{A}$ is just the number of backward messages $|Z_i^-|$ resp. forward messages $|Z_i^+|$; for non-relevant cycles, we have the opposite correspondence. We can therefore rewrite the sum over all columns as

$$\sum_{j=1}^{k} y_j - \sum_{j=1}^{k} y_{k+j} = \sum_{i \in R} \left(|Z_i^-| - |Z_i^+| \right) y_{2k+i} + \sum_{i \in N} \left(|Z_i^+| - |Z_i^-| \right) y_{2k+i}. \tag{5.8}$$

We will first prove that $\bar{\mathbf{y}}^T \mathbf{b} > 0$ for a special type of solutions, called *canonical solutions* $\bar{\mathbf{y}}$, from which we will derive $\mathbf{y}^T \mathbf{b} > 0$ for arbitrary solutions $\mathbf{y}$ later on.

Definition 5.4.5. A canonical solution $\bar{\mathbf{y}}$ must satisfy $\bar{\mathbf{y}} > 0$, with *integer* coefficients, $\bar{\mathbf{y}}^T \mathbf{A} = 0$, and either $\bar{y}_j = 0$ or $\bar{y}_{k+j} = 0$, or both, for all upper-coefficients j of $\bar{\mathbf{y}}$.

Comparing (5.8) with

$$\bar{\mathbf{y}}^T \mathbf{b} = \Xi \sum_{j=1}^{k} \bar{y}_{k+j} - \sum_{j=1}^{k} \bar{y}_j,$$

suggests to consider the linear combination of all rows in the cycle part of $\mathbf{A}$, multiplied with the cycle-coefficients $\bar{\mathbf{y}}^T$, which sum up to the "combined" row vector $\mathbf{s}$: Recalling $\bar{\mathbf{y}}^T \mathbf{A} = 0$, we need to distinguish 2 cases for the upper-coefficients of $\bar{\mathbf{y}}$:

1. If $\bar{y}_{k+j} > 0$ and $\bar{y}_j = 0$, for some upper-coefficient j, then equation (5.7) implies

$$\bar{y}_{k+j} = -s_j > 0.$$

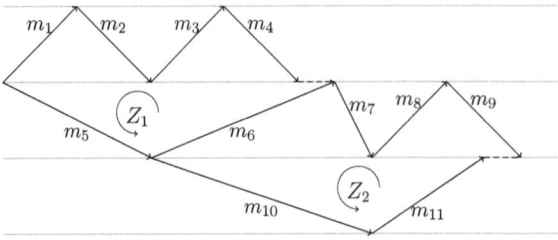

Figure 5.2.: For the relevant cycle Z_1 and the non-relevant cycle Z_2 we have cycle vectors $\mathbf{z_1} = (1, 1, 1, 1, -1, -1, 0, 0, 0, 0, 0)$ and $\mathbf{z_2} = (0, 0, 0, 0, 0, -1, -1, -1, -1, 1, 1)$.

2. If $\bar{y}_j \geqslant 0$ and $\bar{y}_{k+j} = 0$, then
$$\bar{y}_j = s_j \geqslant 0.$$

Hence, we can rewrite condition
$$\bar{\mathbf{y}}^T \mathbf{b} = \Xi \sum_{j=1}^{k} \bar{y}_{k+j} - \sum_{j=1}^{k} \bar{y}_j > 0$$

as
$$\Xi \mathbf{s}^+ + \mathbf{s}^- < 0, \tag{5.9}$$

where $\mathbf{s}^+$ is the sum over all negative coefficients in the sum vector $\mathbf{s}$, while $\mathbf{s}^-$ is the sum over all non-negative coefficients in $\mathbf{s}$. Observe that we have chosen the same notation for the entries of $\mathbf{s}$ as we have used for relevant cycles. This is by no means a coincidence: In fact, if $\mathbf{s}$ represented a relevant cycle, condition (5.9) would immediately follow from the ABC synchrony condition (3.2)[4]. Even though $\mathbf{s}$ is not a cycle vector in general, since its coefficients are usually not in $\{0, \pm 1\}$, we will exploit the fact that $\mathbf{s}$ is always a non-negative integer (since $\bar{\mathbf{y}} > 0$) linear combination of relevant and non-relevant cycles. Since we will prove (5.9) separately for non-negative linear combinations of relevant and non-relevant cycles, we split
$$\Xi \mathbf{s}^+ + \mathbf{s}^- < 0$$

into two parts, i.e.,
$$\Xi \mathbf{s}^+ + \mathbf{s}^- = \Xi \mathbf{s}_R^+ + \mathbf{s}_R^- + \Xi \mathbf{s}_N^- + \mathbf{s}_N^+,$$

---

[4]If $\mathbf{s}$ corresponds to a relevant cycle S, the definition of the cycle vector coefficients yields $|S^-| = \mathbf{s}^-$ and $|S^+| = -\mathbf{s}^+$ and hence $-\Xi \mathbf{s}^+ - \mathbf{s}^- = \Xi |S^+| - |S^-| > 0$ by (3.2).

where $\mathbf{s}_R^+$, $\mathbf{s}_R^-$, $\mathbf{s}_N^+$, $\mathbf{s}_N^-$, are the appropriate restrictions to the index sets R and N. Bear in mind that the sign of the coefficients of non-relevant cycle vectors are opposite to the relevant case.

Lemma 5.4.6 proves (5.9) for the non-relevant part; Lemma 5.4.15 will show the same result for the relevant part.

Lemma 5.4.6 (Non-relevant sum property). *Let $\mathbf{z}_1, \ldots, \mathbf{z}_\ell$, $\ell \geqslant 1$, be cycle vectors representing non-relevant cycles and let $\mathbf{s}_N$ be the vector corresponding to a non-negative linear combination of $\mathbf{z}_1, \ldots, \mathbf{z}_\ell$. Then, it holds that $\Xi \mathbf{s}_N^- + \mathbf{s}_N^+ < 0$.*

Proof. Since, for every i, we have

$$|Z_i^-| - |Z_i^+| \geqslant 0,$$

it follows immediately, by summing up, that every non-negative linear combination $\mathbf{s}_N$ also satisfies

$$|\mathbf{s}_N^-| - |\mathbf{s}_N^+| \geqslant 0.$$

Since $\Xi > 1$, this implies

$$\Xi \mathbf{s}_N^- + \mathbf{s}_N^+ < 0.$$

□

5.4.2. The Cycle Space of the Execution Graph

Proving (5.9) for the relevant part, however, will turn out to be much more involved. The reason for this is that coefficients with opposite sign in a row cancel; this situation occurs for edge e in Figure 3.3, for example. As a consequence, we cannot carry over the ABC synchrony condition (3.2) that holds for every constituent cycle vector to their sum (5.9). In order to solve this problem, we will show that there is a way to get rid of such cancellations, by constructing an equivalent set of cycle vectors that do not have coefficients with opposite sign in any row.

For proving Lemma 5.4.15, we will make use of some non-standard[5] *cycle space* of the underlying execution graph G.

Definition 5.4.7. The cycle space $\mathcal{C}$ of G is the sub-space of the vector space of the edge sets in G over $\mathbb{Q}$ spanned by G's (oriented) cycles.

---

[5] Our "cycle space" is quite different from the well known cycle space in graph theory, cp. (Diestel, 2006), since our notion of "cycles" correspond to cycles in the undirected shadow graph while still taking edge orientation into account.

Since every cycle Z_i corresponds to a unique set of messages in G, which can be uniquely identified by a k-tuple ordered according to the columns in the matrix $\mathbf{A}$, there is a one-to-one correspondence between cycles Z_i in G and the cycle vectors $\mathbf{z}_i$ in $\mathbf{A}$, cp. Figure 5.2. To avoid ambiguities w.r.t. indices, we will usually denote the coefficient for message e in $\mathbf{z}_i$ by $(\mathbf{z}_i)_e$.

Definition 5.4.8. A *cycle space element*

$$Z = \lambda_1 Z_1 \oplus \lambda_2 Z_2 \oplus \cdots \oplus \lambda_\ell Z_\ell$$

is a linear combination of some relevant cycles $Z_1, \ldots, Z_\ell$, with all coefficients $\lambda_i \in \mathbb{Q}$, and the corresponding cycle vector reads

$$\mathbf{z} = \lambda_1 \mathbf{z}_1 + \lambda_2 \mathbf{z}_2 + \cdots + \lambda_\ell \mathbf{z}_\ell.$$

Note that we will use both representations interchangeably in the sequel. The cycle addition operation $\oplus$ is defined as follows: If the cycles Z_1, Z_2 corresponding to the cycle vectors $\mathbf{z}_1$, $\mathbf{z}_2$ are disjoint, i.e.,

$$Z_1 \cap Z_2 = \emptyset,$$

then the cycle space element

$$Z = Z_1 \oplus Z_2 = Z_1 \cup Z_2$$

is the union of the two cycles Z_1, Z_2; it corresponds to the sum of the cycle vectors

$$\mathbf{z} = \mathbf{z}_1 + \mathbf{z}_2.$$

Note that disjoint cycles may have common vertices (and even partially overlapping local edges), but no common messages. If the cycles have a common message e, the outcome of adding $\mathbf{z}_1$ and $\mathbf{z}_2$ depends on the cycle vector orientation of Z_1 and Z_2: If e is *oppositely oriented* in Z_1 and Z_2, formally

$$(\mathbf{z}_1)_e \cdot (\mathbf{z}_2)_e < 0,$$

then the coefficients cancel and hence $(\mathbf{z})_e = 0$. We also say that that e is a *mixed edge*, i.e.,

$$e \in Z_1^- \cap Z_2^+ \text{ or } e \in Z_1^+ \cap Z_2^-$$

in relevant cycles, cp. message e in Figure 3.3. Consequently, e is no longer present in $Z = Z_1 \oplus Z_2$. Otherwise, if e is *identically oriented* in Z_1 and Z_2 (we say that message e is either a forward or a backward edge in both cycles), formally

$$(\mathbf{z}_1)_e \cdot (\mathbf{z}_2)_e > 0,$$

then the coefficients do not cancel and $(\mathbf{z})_e \neq 0$. In this case, e becomes a double-edge in

$$Z = Z_1 \oplus Z_2.$$

Hence, in general, the subgraph $Z = Z_1 \oplus Z_2$ corresponding to $\mathbf{z} = \mathbf{z}_1 + \mathbf{z}_2$ is not a cycle, and

$$(Z_1 \oplus Z_2) = (Z_1 \cup Z_2)$$

is *not* necessarily true. In fact, the general cycle space element

$$Z = \lambda_1 Z_1 \oplus \cdots \oplus \lambda_n Z_n$$

is made up of multi-edges e with arbitrary multiplicity that is,

$$(\mathbf{z})_e = \lambda_1 (\mathbf{z}_1)_e + \cdots + \lambda_n (\mathbf{z}_n)_e \in \mathbb{Q}.$$

We will show, however, that every *non-negative integer* linear combination of cycle vectors representing relevant cycles yields a "relevant cycle-like" vector $\mathbf{z}$, in the sense that its coefficients satisfy the ABC synchrony assumption (3.2). This immediately implies

$$\Xi \mathbf{s}_R^+ + \mathbf{s}_R^- < 0$$

and thus proves (5.9) for the relevant part, see Lemma 5.4.15.

We start with the following Definition 5.4.9 of consistent cycles, which are such that all common edges consistently have either the same or the opposite orientation.

Definition 5.4.9 (Consistent cycles). The cycles Z_1 and Z_2 are *consistent*, if there is some $d \in \{-1, +1\}$ such that the entries in the corresponding cycle vectors satisfy

$$(\mathbf{z}_1)_e \cdot (\mathbf{z}_2)_e = d,$$

for all messages $e \in Z_1 \cap Z_2$. If $d = +1$ resp. $d = -1$, then Z_1 and Z_2 are called *i-consistent* (identically consistent) resp. *o-consistent* (oppositely consistent). If Z_1 and Z_2 are disjoint, then they are i-consistent by definition. A set of cycles $M_1, \ldots, M_n$ is consistent (i-consistent/o-consistent) w.r.t. a cycle Z, if M_i and Z are consistent (i-consistent/o-consistent), for every $1 \leqslant i \leqslant n$.

For convenience, we say that $Z_1 \cap Z_2$ *contains* (resp. *consists of*) oppositely oriented messages, if for some (resp. every) message $e \in Z_1 \cap Z_2$ it holds that

$$(\mathbf{z}_1)_e \cdot (\mathbf{z}_2)_e = -1.$$

We proceed with several technical lemmas devoted to the removal of mixed edges in sums of cycle vectors.

Lemma 5.4.10 (Mixed edge removal (two cycles)). *Let Z_1 and Z_2 be o-consistent cycles, such that all common message chains $m_1, \ldots, m_n$ in $Z_1 \cap Z_2$ consist of oppositely oriented messages only. Then, there are disjoint cycles $M_1, \ldots, M_n$ that are i-consistent w.r.t. both Z_1 and Z_2, such that*

$$Z_1 \oplus Z_2 = M_1 \oplus \cdots \oplus M_n.$$

Moreover,

$$|M_1 \oplus \cdots \oplus M_n| = |Z_1 \oplus Z_2| - 2\sum_{i=1}^{n} |m_i|.$$

Proof. Let

$$Z_1 = v_1 m_1 v_1' \ldots v_2 m_2 v_2' \ldots v_{n-1} m_{n-1} v_{n-1}' \ldots v_n m_n v_n' \ldots v_1,$$

where v_i and v_i' denote the vertices incident to the message chain m_i, be the sequence of vertices and edges of Z_1 listed according to its cycle vector orientation. Since Z_2 traverses all common edges in the opposite direction, its analogous representation reads

$$Z_2 = v_n' m_n v_n \ldots v_{n-1}' m_{n-1} v_{n-1} \ldots v_2' m_2 v_2 \ldots v_1' m_1 v_1 \ldots v_n'.$$

Hence, the chains $m_1, \ldots, m_n$ are cancelled in $Z_1 \oplus Z_2$, only leaving the disjoint cycles

$$M_1 = v_1 \ldots v_n' \ldots v_1,$$
$$M_2 = v_2 \ldots v_1' \ldots v_2,$$
$$\vdots$$
$$M_n = v_n \ldots v_{n-1}' \ldots v_n.$$

Every cycle
$$M_i = v_i \ldots v_{i-1}' \ldots v_i \quad \text{(with } v_0' = v_n'\text{)}$$
consists of exactly one chain of messages $v_{i-1}' \ldots v_i$ in Z_1, and one chain of messages $v_i \ldots v_{i-1}'$ in Z_2, and is hence trivially i-consistent w.r.t. both Z_1 and Z_2. □

Lemma 5.4.11 (Mixed edge removal (single set)). *Let Z be a cycle. If $M_1, \ldots, M_n$ are disjoint cycles such that every M_i and Z are either o-consistent or disjoint, then there is a set of disjoint cycles $M_1' \ldots, M_{l'}'$, all of which are i-consistent w.r.t. Z, such that*

$$M_n \oplus \cdots \oplus M_1 \oplus Z = M_1' \oplus \cdots \oplus M_{l'}'.$$

Proof. We will construct $M_1' \ldots, M_{l'}'$ recursively. For $n = 1$, if Z and M_1 are disjoint (and hence i-consistent by definition), we just set $M_1' = Z$, $M_2' = M_1$ and trivially get

$$M_1 \oplus Z = M_1' \oplus M_2'.$$

Otherwise, Z and M_1 must be o-consistent and the statement of our lemma follows immediately from Lemma 5.4.10, applied to Z and M_1.

Now suppose that we have already constructed a set of disjoint cycles $M_1', \ldots, M_{l'}'$ that are all i-consistent w.r.t. Z with

$$M_{n-1} \oplus \cdots \oplus M_1 \oplus Z = M_1' \oplus \cdots \oplus M_{l'}'.$$

Since $\oplus$ is commutative and associative, it holds that

$$M_n \oplus M_{n-1} \oplus \cdots \oplus M_1 \oplus Z = M_n \oplus M_1' \oplus \cdots \oplus M_{l'}' = M_1' \oplus \ldots \ldots M_{l'}' \oplus M_n.$$

By our hypothesis, every M_ℓ', $1 \leqslant \ell \leqslant l'$, and Z are i-consistent, whereas M_n and Z are either disjoint or o-consistent. It follows immediately that every M_ℓ' and M_n is either o-consistent or disjoint. Since these are exactly the preconditions of our lemma, our recursive construction can be applied again. The termination of this recursive construction is guaranteed, since every application of Lemma 5.4.10 reduces the number of edges in the result. □

Lemma 5.4.12 (Mixed edge removal (general set)). *Let $Z_1, \ldots, Z_n$ be a set of cycles such that, for $1 \leq i < j \leq n$, cycles Z_i and Z_j are either disjoint or o-consistent. Then, there exist disjoint cycles $M_1, \ldots, M_l$ that are all i-consistent w.r.t. every Z_i, $1 \leq i \leq n$, such that*
$$Z_1 \oplus \cdots \oplus Z_n = M_1 \oplus \cdots \oplus M_l.$$

Proof. The proof is by induction. For $n = 1$, Z_1 and $M_1 = Z_1$ are trivially i-consistent, hence establishing the induction base. For the induction step, suppose that there are disjoint cycles $M_1, \ldots, M_l$ that are i-consistent w.r.t. every Z_i, $1 \leq i \leq n-1$, such that
$$Z_1 \oplus \cdots \oplus Z_{n-1} = M_1 \oplus \cdots \oplus M_l.$$

Now, since every M_ℓ, $1 \leq \ell \leq l$, and every Z_i, $1 \leq i \leq n-1$, are i-consistent, whereas every Z_i and Z_n are o-consistent, it follows immediately that every M_ℓ and Z_n is either o-consistent or disjoint. Hence, we can apply Lemma 5.4.11 with $Z = Z_n$, which provides the required set $M'_1 \ldots, M'_{l'}$ of disjoint cycles that are i-consistent w.r.t. every Z_i, $1 \leq i \leq n$ and satisfy
$$M'_1 \oplus \cdots \oplus M'_{l'} = Z_1 \oplus \cdots \oplus Z_n$$

as required. □

Theorem 5.4.13 (*Mixed-free decomposition*)

Let $C \in \mathcal{C}$ be a cycle space element such that
$$C = Z_1 \oplus \cdots \oplus Z_n.$$

Then, there are cycles $M_1, \ldots, M_l$, which are all i-consistent with respect to every Z_i, for $1 \leq i \leq n$, and no $M_j \cap M_{j'}$, for $1 \leq j < j' \leq l$, contains oppositely oriented messages, such that
$$Z_1 \oplus \cdots \oplus Z_n = M_1 \oplus \cdots \oplus M_l.$$

Proof. Let Γ be any non-empty subset of the multi-edges in C, i.e., of messages e that have some integer coefficient

$$(\mathbf{c})_e \notin \{0, \pm 1\}$$

in the cycle vector corresponding to C. We can define an extended cycle space $\mathcal{C}[\Gamma]$ as follows: Given some multi-edge $e \in \Gamma$, there must be at least $k = |(\mathbf{c})_e|$ cycles $Z_{\pi_1}, \ldots, Z_{\pi_k}$ where e has the same orientation

$$d = \operatorname{sgn}((\mathbf{c})_e) = \operatorname{sgn}((\mathbf{z}_{\pi_i})_e) \qquad (1 \leqslant i \leqslant k).$$

For every such Z_{π_i}, we introduce a new edge labeled $e^{Z_{\pi_i}}$ and replace Z_{π_i} by Z'_{π_i}, where $(\mathbf{z}'_{\pi_i})_e = 0$ but $(\mathbf{z}'_{\pi_i})_{e^{Z_{\pi_i}}} = d$. Doing this for all $e \in \Gamma$ provides a new set of cycles

$$Z_1[\Gamma], \ldots, Z_{n^{\Gamma}}[\Gamma] \in \mathcal{C}[\Gamma],$$

which sum up to

$$C[\Gamma] = Z_1[\Gamma] \oplus \cdots \oplus Z_{n^{\Gamma}}[\Gamma].$$

Note that the only difference between C and $C[\Gamma]$ is that we have split all multi-edges $\in \Gamma$ occurring in C into separate new edges (which all have coefficients $\in \{0, \pm 1\}$) in $C[\Gamma]$. Let Γ^* denote the set of *all* multi-edges in C; note that $\Gamma \subset \Gamma^*$ implies that $C[\Gamma]$ still contains multi-edges in $\Gamma^* \backslash \Gamma$.

We will now prove by means of backwards induction on $|\Gamma|$ that the statement of our theorem actually holds for every cycle space element $C[\Gamma]$. Since $C[\emptyset] = C$, this will also prove Theorem 5.4.13.

For the induction base, let $\Gamma = \Gamma^*$. Since all multi-edges have been split in $C[\Gamma^*]$, every pair $Z_i[\Gamma^*]$, $Z_j[\Gamma^*]$, for $1 \leqslant i < j \leqslant n^{\Gamma^*}$, is either disjoint or o-consistent. Lemma 5.4.12 thus reveals that there are disjoint cycles

$$M_1[\Gamma^*], \ldots, M_k[\Gamma^*] \in \mathcal{C}[\Gamma^*]$$

that are all i-consistent w.r.t. every $Z_i[\Gamma^*]$, where

$$M_1[\Gamma^*] \oplus \cdots \oplus M_k[\Gamma^*] = Z_1[\Gamma^*] \oplus \cdots \oplus Z_{n^{\Gamma^*}}[\Gamma^*]$$

as required. Note that no $M_i[\Gamma^*] \cap M_j[\Gamma^*]$ can contain oppositely oriented messages because they are disjoint.

For the induction step, we assume that there are cycles

$$M'_1[\Gamma], \ldots, M'_k[\Gamma] \in \mathcal{C}[\Gamma],$$

which are all i-consistent w.r.t. every $Z_i[\Gamma]$, $1 \leqslant i \leqslant n^\Gamma$ and no $M'_j[\Gamma] \cap M'_{j'}[\Gamma]$, for $1 \leqslant j < j' \leqslant k$, contains oppositely oriented messages, such that

$$M'_1[\Gamma] \oplus \cdots \oplus M'_k[\Gamma] = C[\Gamma].$$

Let $M'_j[\Gamma]$, for $1 \leqslant j \leqslant k$, be such a cycle. Suppose that $M'_j[\Gamma]$ contains $\alpha \geqslant 1$ "instances" of a multi-chain $c \subseteq \Gamma$, i.e., α maximum-length chains $c^{Z_1}, \ldots, c^{Z_\alpha}$ which have all been obtained by introducing new edges for the multi-edges making up the *single* multi-chain c. W.l.o.g., we can write

$$M'_j[\Gamma] = v_1^{Z_1} c^{Z_1} v_2^{Z_1} \ldots v_1^{Z_2} c^{Z_2} v_2^{Z_2} \ldots v_1^{Z_\alpha} c^{Z_\alpha} v_2^{Z_\alpha} \ldots v_1^{Z_1}.$$

Consequently, we have the following chains in $M'_j[\Gamma]$:

$$v_1^{Z_1} c^{Z_1} v_2^{Z_1} \ldots v_1^{Z_2} c^{Z_2} = M_{j_1} c^{Z_2},$$
$$v_1^{Z_2} c^{Z_2} v_2^{Z_2} \ldots v_1^{Z_3} c^{Z_3} = M_{j_2} c^{Z_3},$$
$$\vdots$$
$$v_1^{Z_\alpha} c^{Z_\alpha} v_2^{Z_\alpha} \ldots v_1^{Z_1} c^{Z_1} = M_{j_\alpha} c^{Z_1}.$$

Now, if we rejoin all the edges in $c^{Z_1}, \ldots, c^{Z_\alpha}$ to form the multi-chain c again, that is, if we make a transition from $\mathcal{C}[\Gamma]$ to $\mathcal{C}[\Gamma \backslash c]$, then all instances of $c^{Z_1}, \ldots, c^{Z_\alpha}$ in the above chains collapse to the single multi-chain c. Consequently, in $\mathcal{C}[\Gamma \backslash c]$, every of the M_{j_ℓ}, $1 \leqslant \ell \leqslant \alpha$, above actually forms a *cycle* $M_{j_\ell}[\Gamma \backslash c]$—note that the vertices $v_1^{Z_\ell}$ and $v_1^{Z_{\ell+1}}$ also collapse to a single vertex. Since $M'_j[\Gamma]$ is i-consistent w.r.t. every $Z_i[\Gamma]$, $1 \leqslant i \leqslant n^\Gamma$, every $M_{j_\ell}[\Gamma \backslash c]$ must be i-consistent w.r.t. every $Z_i[\Gamma \backslash c]$, $1 \leqslant i \leqslant n^{\Gamma \backslash c}$, as well. Furthermore, according to the construction above, every edge of $M'_j[\Gamma]$ (except the edges in $c^{Z_1}, \ldots, c^{Z_\alpha}$, of course) is contained in exactly one cycle $M_{j_\ell}[\Gamma \backslash c]$, and no $M_{j_\ell}[\Gamma \backslash c] \cap M_{j_{\ell'}}[\Gamma \backslash c]$ can contain oppositely oriented edges. Finally, no

$$M_{i_\ell}[\Gamma \backslash c] \cap M_{j_{\ell'}}[\Gamma \backslash c],$$

for $i \neq j$, can contain oppositely oriented edges either, since $M'_j[\Gamma]$ and $M'_i[\Gamma]$ are disjoint. Hence, taking all the sets $M_{j_\ell}[\Gamma \backslash c]$ (or, if $\alpha = 0$ for $M'_j[\Gamma]$, then $M_j[\Gamma \backslash c] := M'_j[\Gamma]$) provides the sought set

$$M_1[\Gamma \backslash c], \ldots, M_k[\Gamma \backslash c] \in \mathcal{C}[\Gamma \backslash c],$$

thereby completing our proof. □

Corollary 5.4.14. *Let $C \in \mathcal{C}$ be such that $C = Z_1 \oplus \cdots \oplus Z_n$, for relevant cycles $Z_1, \ldots, Z_n$. Then, $\frac{|C^-|}{|C^+|} < \Xi$.*

Proof. Applying Theorem 5.4.13 yields cycles $M_1, \ldots, M_l$ such that

$$C = Z_1 \oplus \cdots \oplus Z_n = M_1 \oplus \cdots \oplus M_l,$$

which do not contain oppositely oriented messages that would cancel when summing up. In order to prove $\frac{|C^-|}{|C^+|} < \Xi$, it hence suffices to show $\frac{|M_i^-|}{|M_i^+|} < \Xi$ for every M_i. There are only two possibilities:

1. $M_i^- \subseteq C^-, M_i^+ \subseteq C^+$: If M_i is relevant, then obviously

$$\frac{|M_i^-|}{|M_i^+|} < \Xi.$$

Assume, for the sake of contradiction, that M_i is non-relevant. Then there is a local edge $\kappa \in M_i$ that is traversed forward (causally) in M_i, and hence in C. Since

$$C = Z_1 \oplus \cdots \oplus Z_n,$$

there must be some Z_j with $\kappa \in Z_j$ where κ is traversed in the same way as in C and, hence, in M_i. This contradicts Z_j being a relevant cycle, however.

2. $M_i^+ \subseteq C^-, M_i^- \subseteq C^+$: By (3.1), it holds that $|M_i^-| \geqslant |M_i^+|$ and hence

$$\frac{|M_i^+|}{|M_i^-|} \leqslant 1 < \Xi.$$

Since M_i^- resp. M^+ correspond to edges in C^+ resp. C^-, it follows that M_i contributes properly to $\frac{|C^-|}{|C^+|} < \Xi$ as required. Note that this holds independently of whether M_i is relevant or not.

This completes the proof of Corollary 5.4.14. □

As a consequence, we finally get the desired proof of (5.9) for the relevant part:

Lemma 5.4.15 (Relevant sum property). *Let $z_1, \ldots, z_\ell$ be cycle vectors representing relevant cycles and let s_R be the vector corresponding to a non-negative integer linear combination of $z_1, \ldots, z_\ell$. Then, it holds that $\Xi s_R^+ + s_R^- < 0$.*

Proof. Corollary 5.4.14 does not require the Z_i to be distinct. Since

$$S_R = \lambda_1 Z_1 \oplus \cdots \oplus \lambda_\ell Z_\ell$$

for non-negative integer coefficients λ_i, we can hence invoke Corollary 5.4.14 with λ_i instances of the same relevant cycle Z_i, for $1 \leqslant i \leqslant \ell$. □

Combining Lemma 5.4.6 and Lemma 5.4.15 immediately proves that every canonical solution $\bar{y}$ (see Definition 5.4.5) satisfies $\bar{y}^T b > 0$. It only remains to extend this result to arbitrary solution vectors y, which is done in the following Theorem 5.4.16:

Theorem 5.4.16 (*Existence of a normalized assignment*)

> *The system $Ax < b$ corresponding to a finite execution graph has always a solution, and hence a normalized assignment.*

Proof. The statement follows immediately from Theorem 5.4.4, if we can show that every $y > 0$ with coefficients $y_j \in \mathbb{Q}$ satisfying $y^T A = 0$ also fulfills $y^T b > 0$. If y is a canonical solution $\bar{y}$, then $\bar{y}^T b > 0$ follows from adding the results of Lemma 5.4.6 and Lemma 5.4.15, recall (5.9) in conjunction with

$$\Xi s^+ + s^- = \Xi s_R^+ + s_R^- + \Xi s_N^- + s_N^+.$$

Otherwise, we can derive a canonical solution $\bar{y}$ from a non-canonical solution y as follows:

1. For all upper-coefficients $1 \leqslant j \leqslant k$ of y: If $y_j > y_{k+j}$, then $\bar{y}_j = y_j - y_{k+j}$ and $\bar{y}_{k+j} = 0$; otherwise, $\bar{y}_{k+j} = y_{k+j} - y_j$ and $\bar{y}_j = 0$.

2. For all cycle-coefficients $2k+1 \leqslant i \leqslant 2k+l+m$ of y: $\bar{y}_i = y_i$.

3. Finally, multiply every $\bar{y}_j$ by the least common multiple of $\bar{y}_1, \ldots, \bar{y}_{2k+l+m}$ to get integer coefficients.

Since $\mathbf{y}^T\mathbf{A} = 0$, it follows immediately from the above definition of $\bar{\mathbf{y}}$ that $\bar{\mathbf{y}}^T\mathbf{A} = 0$. Hence, $\bar{\mathbf{y}}^T\mathbf{b} > 0$. Now consider $(\mathbf{y}^T - \bar{\mathbf{y}}^T)\mathbf{b}^T$; after cancelling the common parts of $\bar{\mathbf{y}}$ and $\mathbf{y}$, according to our construction, we get

$$(\mathbf{y}^T - \bar{\mathbf{y}}^T)\mathbf{b}^T = \sum_{j:y_{k+j} \geqslant y_j} (\Xi - 1)\, y_j + \sum_{j:y_j > y_{k+j}} (\Xi - 1)\, y_{k+j}.$$

This term is non-negative, since $\mathbf{y}$ is non-negative and $\Xi > 1$. Hence,

$$\mathbf{y}^T\mathbf{b} \geqslant \bar{\mathbf{y}}^T\mathbf{b} > 0$$

and we are done. □

Theorem 5.4.16 immediately implies the sought Theorem 5.3.1.

5.5. Discussion

In this chapter we have presented a non-trivial model indistinguishability argument where our main purpose was to show the existence of an end-to-end delay assignment of the execution graph of a run in the ABC model that is compatible with the Θ-Model. While the presented proof is not constructive—recall that Theorem 5.4.4 only guarantees that a solution *exists*—we could nevertheless easily obtain such an end-to-end assignment by running a linear programming algorithm on our system of linear inequalities, if needed.

Part of our future work is devoted to finding other applications where such a causality preserving space-time transformation might be of use.

Below Consensus Solvability

Chapter 6

Almost Asynchronous System Models

IN THIS CHAPTER we will focus on the lower end of the model hierarchy depicted in Figure 1.2 (Page 21). More specifically, we will introduce two *very* weak system models, $\mathcal{M}^{\text{anti}}$ and $\mathcal{M}^{\text{sink}}$, that are close to the asynchronous model ($\mathcal{M}^{\text{ASYNC}}$) of Fischer et al. (1985), with respect to inclusion of admissible runs and therefore also problem solvability power. [1] Nevertheless, we will show that $\mathcal{M}^{\text{anti}}$ and $\mathcal{M}^{\text{sink}}$ are non-trivial restrictions of $\mathcal{M}^{\text{ASYNC}}$, by proving that $(n-1)$-set agreement—the weakest instance of the generalized agreement problem—is solvable in our models.[2] We will not show this result by providing a set agreement algorithm, but rather by implementing the weakest failure detector $\mathcal{L}$ (see Delporte-Gallet et al., 2008) for set agreement.

6.1. Weak System Models for Set Agreement

In this section, we introduce two system models $\mathcal{M}^{\text{anti}}$ and $\mathcal{M}^{\text{sink}}$ with very weak synchrony conditions. By implementing $\mathcal{L}$ in both of these models, we show that they are strong enough to solve set agreement. In order to allow this, we need to restrict the set of admissible runs of $\mathcal{M}^{\text{ASYNC}}$ by adding some—albeit very weak—synchrony conditions. While set agreement is solvable in either one of these models, the partial synchrony-like assumptions of $\mathcal{M}^{\text{sink}}$ are fundamentally different from the time-free message-ordering properties of model $\mathcal{M}^{\text{anti}}$.

---

[1] The content of this chapter originated from joint work with Martin Biely (see Biely et al., 2009a).
[2] Recall that $(n-1)$-set agreement (also known as "set agreement") is impossible in the purely asynchronous model (see Section 1.4).

We first present the formal definition of $\mathcal{L}$ (see Delporte-Gallet et al., 2008); we assume that the reader is familiar with the notion of a *failure detector* (see Chandra and Toueg, 1996), which we formally introduce in Section 7.2.

Definition 6.1.1. The *loneliness detector* $\mathcal{L}$ outputs either TRUE or FALSE, such that for all environments $\mathcal{E}$ and for all failure patterns $F \in \mathcal{E}$ the following hold:

$$\exists p \in \Pi \ \forall t \colon H(p,t) = \text{FALSE} \tag{6.1}$$

$$|F| = n-1 \implies \exists q \notin F \ \exists t \ \forall t' \geqslant t \colon H(q,t') = \text{TRUE} \tag{6.2}$$

Essentially, the conditions of Definition 6.1.1 require the existence of some (possibly faulty) process that never outputs TRUE, and that, in the case that all but one process crash, the remaining process "detects" its loneliness by outputting TRUE.

6.1.1. The model $\mathcal{M}^{\text{anti}}$

Analogously as for the ABC model presented in Chapter 3, we consider a set Π of n distributed processes, which communicate via message passing over a fully connected point-to-point network. Model $\mathcal{M}^{\text{anti}}$ is—just like the ABC model—a message-driven execution model where computing steps are triggered by the arrival of messages instead of the passage of time. Inspired by the round-trip-based model introduced by Mostefaoui et al. (2003, 2004), we specify our synchrony requirements as conditions on the order of round-trip message arrivals. In this model computations proceed in *asynchronous rounds*: At the start of a round, every process p sends a ($query$)-message to all processes, including itself. If a process receives a ($query$)-message from some process q, it replies by sending a ($resp$)-message to q. When p has received at least $n - f$ ($resp$)-messages, it *starts a new round*, by sending out another ($query$)-message to all processes. Since we aim at $(n-1)$-set agreement with $f = n - 1$ here, processes hence start their new round after receiving just 1 response. In the case where all other processes crash, the remaining process will end up receiving only messages sent by itself.

Definition 6.1.2 (Anti source). Let p be a correct or faulty process. Process p is an *anti source*, if, whenever p sends a query to all processes, then the response from some other (possibly changing) process arrives at p before process p starts a new round.

Intuitively speaking, an anti source is an (unknown) process whose round-trips with itself are never the fastest. Note that this definition also implies that the anti source can never be the last remaining correct process. Figure 6.1 on Page 83 shows an example execution where process p is an anti source.

Definition 6.1.3. Let α be a run of a distributed algorithm. Then, α is *admissible in* $\mathcal{M}^{anti}$ if the following holds:

1. Processes perform message-driven computation in α and α is admissible in $\mathcal{M}^{ASYNC}$ (see Definition 2.3.1 on Page 25).

2. At least one process is an anti source in α.

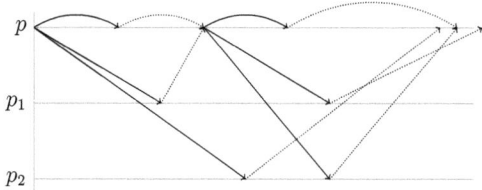

Figure 6.1.: An execution of an algorithm in model $\mathcal{M}^{anti}$ where process p is an anti source. Note that p needs to send $(resp)$-messages even in reply to $(query)$-messages sent by itself. Reply messages are depicted as dotted lines. For the sake of readability, $(query)$-messages sent by p_1 and p_2 were omitted.

6.1.2. Implementing $\mathcal{L}$ in Model $\mathcal{M}^{anti}$.

Algorithm 3 provides an implementation of the loneliness failure detector $\mathcal{L}$ in $\mathcal{M}^{anti}$. Note that, since $\mathcal{M}^{anti}$ is a message-driven model, the intuition behind Algorithm 3 is fairly easy to understand: A process sets its $output_\mathcal{L}$ to TRUE if and only if it receives its own reply to its round-trip first. In every run, the anti source p will always receive the reply message from *some* other process first and therefore never changes its variable $output_\mathcal{L}$ to TRUE.

Theorem 6.1.4

Failure detector $\mathcal{L}$ is implementable in model $\mathcal{M}^{anti}$.

Proof. Let p be an anti source in a run of Algorithm 3. At the start of every round, process p sends a $(query)$-message to all other processes. By the definition of an anti source, p always receives a $(resp)$-message to its query from some process $q \neq p$ as its

---
Algorithm 3 Implementing $\mathcal{L}$ in Model $\mathcal{M}^{\text{anti}}$

Variables:
1: $\mathit{output}_\mathcal{L}, \mathit{alone} \in \{\text{TRUE}, \text{FALSE}\}$

Initially:
2: $\mathit{output}_\mathcal{L} \leftarrow \text{FALSE}$;
3: $\mathit{startRound}()$

4: **upon** rcv (resp) from process q **do**
5:   **if** $p \neq q$ **then**
6:     $\mathit{alone} \leftarrow \text{FALSE}$
7:   **if** $\mathit{alone} = \text{FALSE}$ **then**
8:     $\mathit{startRound}()$
9:   **else**
10:     $\mathit{output}_\mathcal{L} \leftarrow \text{TRUE}$

11: **upon** receive (query) from q **do**
12:   send (resp) do q

13: **procedure** $\mathit{startRound}()$
14:   $\mathit{alone} \leftarrow \text{TRUE}$
15:   send (query) to all
---

first reply. Process p will therefore pass the test in Line 5 and set $\mathit{alone} \leftarrow \text{FALSE}$. It follows that p will always pass the test in Line 7 and therefore $\mathit{output}_\mathcal{L}$ remains FALSE forever, which proves Property (6.1).

To show Property (6.2), we consider the case where q is the only correct process in α. Then there is a time after which q does not receive any more messages from other processes. That is, there is a time t such that whenever q sends out a (query)-message, it only receives its own response, hence, it never sets $\mathit{alone} \leftarrow \text{FALSE}$ at any time $t' \geqslant t$. The one (resp) message that q receives, however, is sufficient to subsequently cause q to set $\mathit{output}_\mathcal{L}$ to TRUE in Line 10. □

6.1.3. The Model $\mathcal{M}^{\text{sink}}$

The model $\mathcal{M}^{\text{sink}}$ is a time-driven model, similarly to the weak-timely link (WTL) models (Aguilera et al., 2004, 2003; Malkhi et al., 2005; Hutle et al., 2009) that we have introduced in Section 1.3. Essentially, the WTL models assume that processes are partially synchronous (Dwork et al., 1988) while trying to minimize the synchrony requirements on communication delays.

In the model $\mathcal{M}^{anti}$, there was no bound on the duration of a round-trip as only the order of the arrival of messages mattered. Our second model $\mathcal{M}^{sink}$ enforces a similar order by means of explicit communication delay bounds and message timeouts, like the WTL models. A simple approach would be to assume a bound on the round trip time, which is essentially equivalent to requiring a moving bi-directional link from one process. Note that this assumption would make one process permanently 1-*accessible* (in the notation of Malkhi et al. (2005)), which is unnecessarily strong for implementing $\mathcal{L}$. Analogously to the WTL models, we restrict the power of computing steps by requiring that a process can *either* receive a (possibly empty!) set of messages or send messages to an arbitrary set of processes, but not both.

While we did not use the discrete global clock T that we introduced in Chapter 2 for the analysis of our message-driven models (i.e., the ABC model and model $\mathcal{M}^{anti}$), we will make heavy use of it throughout the following section. Like Dwork et al. (1988), we assume two bounds Φ and Δ, where Φ bounds the relative speed of processes, whereas Δ bounds the transmission delay of a timely message m, i.e., the number of steps of processes take during the transmission of m. We say that a message m is delivered *timely* over the link (p,q) iff it is sent by p at time t and received by q not later than in the first reception step taken by q at (or after) time $t + \Delta$. Note that this definition implies that all messages sent to a crashed process (or a process that crashes before taking the decisive reception step) are considered to be delivered timely.

As in the WTL models (and in contrast to (Dwork et al., 1988)), we do *not* require Δ to hold for all messages. Rather, we base our synchrony conditions on the notion of a sink, which is a process q that can always receive some messages timely (see below).

Definition 6.1.5 (Sink). A process q is a *sink in a run* α if there is a correct process p such any message sent from p to q before q has possibly crashed, is delivered timely to q.

Note that we only consider p to be correct here to keep the definition simple. In case the sink q crashes, the sender p may crash as well, as long as it does so after q. Note that this is actually the decisive difference between q being a sink and p being a perpetual 1-source (in the notation of Aguilera et al. (2003)), which in contrast must always be a correct process. However, this synchrony requirement can be weakened even further, if we restrict our attention to algorithms with a "round like" structure—that is, algorithms where each process repeatedly sends messages to all other processes, as it is often the case for heartbeat-based failure detector implementations. For such algorithms, one could also use the following Definition 6.1.5, where the timely process p may change. In contrast to the timely f-source model with moving timely links of Hutle et al. (2009), however, we cannot rely on a single (send-)event as a common reference point in the definition.

Definition 6.1.6 (Sink'). A process q is a *sink in a run* α if, for every $i \geqslant 1$, there is a (possibly changing) process p such that the i-th message sent by p to q is delivered timely to q.

Note carefully that, since all messages sent to crashed processes are by definition delivered timely, a sink can also be an initially faulty process.

Definition 6.1.7 (Model $\mathcal{M}^{\text{sink}}$). Let α be a run of a distributed algorithm. Then, α is *admissible in* $\mathcal{M}^{sink}$ if the following holds:

1. Run α is admissible in $\mathcal{M}^{\text{ASYNC}}$ and processes perform time-driven computation.

2. There is a bound Φ, such that in every interval of Φ ticks of T, every process that is alive throughout the interval takes at least one step.

3. At least one process is a sink in α.

At a first glance, it might be surprising that model $\mathcal{M}^{\text{sink}}$ is a perpetual model, i.e., a model where all model properties must hold at all times. This is necessary in order to implement $\mathcal{L}$ (see Definition 6.1.1), which itself is a non-eventual failure detector. In fact, this is no peculiarity of set agreement: The weakest failure detector for $n-1$ resilient consensus is $\langle \Sigma, \Omega \rangle$, which has also perpetual properties (see Delporte-Gallet et al., 2010).

Moreover, the definition of $\mathcal{L}$ makes it necessary that at least one process never falsely suspects "loneliness", i.e., the model parameters Φ and Δ must be known and hold right from the start. While it would be sufficient if only the sink knew the real model parameters Φ and Δ, we do not assume that a process knows whether or not it is the sink in a particular run.

6.1.4. Implementing $\mathcal{L}$ in Model $\mathcal{M}^{\text{sink}}$.

Algorithm 4 on Page 87 shows a simple protocol that implements $\mathcal{L}$ in model $\mathcal{M}^{\text{sink}}$: Variable $output_\mathcal{L}$ contains the simulated failure detector output. Every process p periodically sends out (*alive, phase*)-messages that carry the current phase-counter *phase*. In addition, it sets a timer that is implemented using simple step counting. If p does not receive a timely (*alive, ph'*)-message that was sent by some other process in the current (or a future) phase, it sets $output_{\mathcal{L}} \leftarrow$ TRUE in Line 16. Note that in this case the timer is not restarted; the algorithm continues to send (*alive, phase*)-messages to the other processes, however. Clearly Algorithm 4 would also work in an *anonymous* system (see Attiya et al., 1988; Angluin, 1980), where processes do not have unique identifiers but can only distinguish their neighbors via local port numbers.

Algorithm 4 Implementing $\mathcal{L}$ in Model $\mathcal{M}^{\text{sink}}$

   Variables:
1: $output_{\mathcal{L}} \in \{\text{TRUE}, \text{FALSE}\}$
2: $phase, maxSeen \in \mathbb{Z}$

   Initially:
3: $output_{\mathcal{L}} \leftarrow$ FALSE
4: $phase \leftarrow -1$
5: $maxSeen \leftarrow -1$
6: $startPhase()$

7: **every** η steps **do:**
8:    $startPhase()$

9: **upon** receive (*alive, ph'*) **do**
10:    $maxSeen \leftarrow \max(maxSeen, ph')$
11: **upon** expiration of *timer* **do**
12:    **if** $maxSeen \geqslant phase$ **then**
13:      $timer \leftarrow \Phi\eta + \Delta$
14:      start *timer*
15:    **else**
16:      $output_{\mathcal{L}} \leftarrow$ TRUE

17: **procedure** $startPhase()$
18:    $phase \leftarrow phase + 1$
19:    send (*alive, phase*) to all remote processes

We now prove the correctness of Algorithm 4. The following lemma shows that the emulated $\mathcal{L}$ at a sink never outputs TRUE:

Lemma 6.1.8. *If process q is a sink, then q never executes Line 16 of Algorithm 4.*

Proof. We must show that q receives the $(alive, k)$-message from some process before its timer runs out the $(k+1)$-st time, for any $k \geq 0$. Since q is a sink, the $(alive, k)$ is delivered timely to q from some process p. Let $T(\psi)$ denote the time on our global clock T when event ψ takes place somewhere in the system. Suppose that p sends the $(alive, k)$-message in some step ψ_p. By the code of the algorithm and the simultaneous initial start-up, process p must have executed $k\eta$ steps. Since processes are partially synchronous, we have

$$T(\psi_p) \leq \Phi k \eta.$$

Now suppose that q's timer expires in step ψ_q for the $(k+1)$-st time. That is, q has made $(k+1)(\Phi\eta + \Delta)$ steps by ψ_q. Obviously, we have

$$T(\psi_q) \geq (k+1)(\Phi\eta + \Delta).$$

Considering that the message from p to q is delivered timely, we are done if we can show

$$T(\psi_p) + \Delta \leq T(\psi_q).$$

We find that for all $k \geq 0$ it holds that

$$\begin{aligned} T(\psi_p) + \Delta &\leq k\Phi\eta + \Delta \\ &< (k+1)\Phi\eta + \Delta \\ &\leq (k+1)(\Phi\eta + \Delta) \\ &\leq T(\psi_q), \end{aligned}$$

which completes the proof. □

Theorem 6.1.9

Algorithm 4 implements failure detector $\mathcal{L}$ in model $\mathcal{M}^{sink}$ for $f = n - 1$.

Proof. Let α be a run of Algorithm 4 in $\mathcal{M}^{sink}$, and p be any sink. Lemma 6.1.8 implies that p perpetually outputs FALSE in α, so (6.1) holds.

For proving (6.2), suppose that $n - 1$ processes crash in α. Since there must be some process from which the sink p receives timely messages, p cannot be the only correct process in α. Let $q \neq p$ be the only correct process in α. Since q only sends its *alive*-messages to remote processes and no other process is alive, q's timer will eventually

expire without receiving any message, Therefore, q will set $output_\mathcal{L} \leftarrow$ TRUE in Line 16.
□

6.2. Consensus Impossibility

So far, we have shown that our models are strong enough to solve set agreement. This fact alone, however, is of little use, since we could have done the same in one of the existing models for consensus. To show that our results have merit, we will prove that consensus is impossible in our models. Due to the fact that our models are very close to the asynchronous model, the proof is surprisingly simple.

Theorem 6.2.1

Consider a message passing system of size $n \geqslant 3$, where up to $n-1$ processes may fail by crashing. There is no algorithm that solves consensus in model $\mathcal{M}^{anti}$ or in model $\mathcal{M}^{sink}$.

Proof. Suppose, for the sake of a contradiction, that there is an algorithm A^{sink} (resp. A^{anti}) that solves consensus in model $\mathcal{M}^{sink}$ (resp. $\mathcal{M}^{anti}$).

$\mathcal{M}^{sink}$: Consider a run α of A^{sink} where some process p is initially dead. Since p satisfies the definition of a sink, there are no other synchrony requirements on the links connecting the remaining correct processes. Hence the set of the runs where p is initially dead is indistinguishable from the set of runs generated by A^{sink} in a system $\mathcal{M}^{ASYNC}$ with just $n-1 \geqslant 2$ processes, where processes are partially synchronous, all links are asynchronous, and $f = n - 2 \geqslant 1$ processes can still crash. This contradicts the impossibility results of Dolev et al. (1987, Table 1).

$\mathcal{M}^{anti}$: Consider a run α of A^{anti}, where some process p is initially dead. Since p satisfies the definition of an anti source, there are no other synchrony requirements at all in $\mathcal{M}^{anti}$. Therefore, the set of these runs where p is initially dead is indistinguishable from the set of runs generated by A^{anti} in a system $\mathcal{M}^{ASYNC}$ with $n - 1 \geqslant 2$ processes, where still $f = n - 2 \geqslant 1$ processes can crash. This, however, contradicts the FLP impossibility (Fischer et al., 1985). □

While Theorem 6.2.1 states the important impossibility of consensus for our models, we can show an even tighter bound for $\mathcal{M}^{anti}$:

Corollary 6.2.2. There is no algorithm that solves $(n-2)$-set agreement in $\mathcal{M}^{anti}$, for $n \geqslant 3$.

Proof. In the proof of Theorem 6.2.1 we show that $\mathcal{M}^{\text{anti}}$ is equivalent to the asynchronous system $\mathcal{M}^{\text{ASYNC}}$ with $n-1$ processes, of which $n-2$ can crash. Applying the k-set agreement impossibility (Saks and Zaharoglou, 2000; Borowsky and Gafni, 1993; Herlihy and Shavit, 1993) to this system completes the proof. □

6.3. Comparing $\mathcal{M}^{\text{sink}}$ to an f-Source Model

It is interesting to compare $\mathcal{M}^{\text{sink}}$ to the f-source model $\vec{\mathcal{S}}_{f*}$ of Hutle et al. (2009), which is strong enough to solve consensus by implementing the leader oracle Ω. Failure detector[3] Ω eventually outputs the id of a correct process at every process, and was shown to be sufficient for solving consensus in an asynchronous system when no more than $f < n/2$ processes fail by crashing (see Chandra and Toueg, 1996; Chandra et al., 1996).

Just like $\mathcal{M}^{\text{sink}}$, model $\vec{\mathcal{S}}_{f*}$ assumes that processes are partially synchronous and that processes can send a message to multiple receivers in a single step. Moreover, in every run that is admissible in $\vec{\mathcal{S}}_{f*}$, there is some correct process p that is an eventual moving-f-source. This means that eventually p has at least f outgoing timely links, i.e., messages are delivered timely, to a (possibly changing!) set of f processes.

Since we consider a perpetual model $\mathcal{M}^{\text{sink}}$, with wait-free failure patterns where up to $n-1$ processes can crash, we will compare $\mathcal{M}^{\text{sink}}$ to a perpetual model $\vec{\mathcal{S}}_{n-1*}$ that contains at least one *perpetual* moving-$(n-1)$-source p. Clearly, since $f = n-1$ comprises all remote processes, there is no difference between a moving and non-moving source in this scenario, as the timely links are fixed. Since every process $q \neq p$ receives all messages from p timely, every such process q is in fact a sink. Hence, it is not difficult to show that $\mathcal{M}^{\text{sink}}$ has weaker synchrony requirements than $\vec{\mathcal{S}}_{n-1*}$.

Theorem 6.3.1

Any run α that is admissible in the (perpetual) model $\vec{\mathcal{S}}_{n-1*}$ is admissible in $\mathcal{M}^{\text{sink}}$, but there are runs admissible in $\mathcal{M}^{\text{sink}}$ that are not admissible in $\vec{\mathcal{S}}_{n-1*}$.

Proof. The first part of the theorem is immediate from the previous discussion. To see that there are runs that are only admissible in $\mathcal{M}^{\text{sink}}$ but not in $\vec{\mathcal{S}}_{n-1*}$, consider, for example, the run α where the (only!) sink is initially dead. As there are no other synchrony requirements on any remaining messages in α, the existence of a timely $(n-1)$-source is not guaranteed. □

---
[3] We formally introduce failure detectors in Chapter 7.

Reliability of Communication Links

In $\mathcal{S}_{f*}^{\rightarrow}$, links are assumed to be reliable as in $\mathcal{M}^{\text{sink}}$, but it is argued by Hutle et al. (2009) that this assumption is unnecessary. In the work by Aguilera et al. (2003) and Malkhi et al. (2005) on weak system models for implementing Ω, links can be unreliable. This leads us to the question of whether we could drop the reliable links assumption for model $\mathcal{M}^{\text{sink}}$ as well. In fact, we can answer this question in the affirmative: If we are only interested in implementing $\mathcal{L}$ in $\mathcal{M}^{\text{sink}}$, it suffices that all messages sent over a timely link arrive; all other links may be totally unreliable.

6.4. Discussion

In this chapter we have introduced two weak system models that are just strong enough to solve the weakest instance of the set agreement problem. The WTL models, to which our model $\mathcal{M}^{\text{sink}}$ belongs, are frequently employed for finding weak(est) system models for consensus, as we have discussed previously in Section 1.5.

From the perspective of searching for a weakest model for set agreement, we conjecture that our synchrony conditions are not only sufficient but also necessary, since our models hold even if all but one process are unable to obtain anything more than local knowledge of the system. Loosening this requirement would mean that processes are unable to perform any sort of failure detection, which makes it unlikely that there is a WTL model for set agreement that is substantially weaker than $\mathcal{M}^{\text{sink}}$.

Chapter 7

The Generalized Loneliness Detector $\mathcal{L}(k)$

> All generalizations are
> dangerous, even this one.
>
> (Alexandre Dumas père)

IN THIS CHAPTER we will introduce our generalization of the loneliness detector $\mathcal{L}$ (Delporte-Gallet et al., 2008) and show that it is sufficient for solving k-set agreement. Instead of detecting loneliness, $\mathcal{L}(k)$ provides information on "$(n-k)$-loneliness". Intuitively speaking, the output of $\mathcal{L}(k)$ can be used by some correct process to eventually detect the case where at least k processes have crashed.[1]

We will also discuss various relationships between $\mathcal{L}(k)$ and existing failure detectors for k-set agreement in non-anonymous and anonymous settings.

7.1. k-Set Agreement

The *k-set agreement* problem was introduced by Chaudhuri (1993) as a generalization of the consensus problem (see Section 1.4). Every process p starts with a proposal value v and must eventually and irrevocably decide on some value adhering to the following three constraints:

k-Agreement: Processes must decide on at most k different values.

---
[1] The $\mathcal{L}(k)$ failure detector was developed in joint work with Martin Biely (see Biely et al., 2009a).

Validity: If a process decides on v, then v was proposed by some process.

Termination: Every correct process must eventually decide.

Note that the k-set agreement problem was shown to be impossible in the asynchronous system model (see Borowsky and Gafni, 1993; Herlihy and Shavit, 1993; Saks and Zaharoglou, 2000)) if $f \geqslant k$ processes can crash.

7.2. Failure Detectors

In Chapter 6 we have shown how to simulate the output of a failure detector in a partially synchronous system. We will now formally introduce failure detectors in the context of asynchronous system.

Throughout this section we assume the model $\mathcal{M}^{\text{ASYNC}}$ (see Chapter 2) without any additional synchrony requirements. A failure detector (see Chandra and Toueg, 1996) $\mathcal{D}$ is an oracle that can be queried by processes in any step, before making a state transition. The behaviour of $\mathcal{D}$ in a run α depends on the failure pattern F (see Chapter 2), which defines the set of admissible *failure detector histories*. The value of a query of a process p in a step at time t is defined by the *history function* $H(p, t)$, which maps process identifiers and time to the *range* of output symbols of $\mathcal{D}$.

We denote the augmented asynchronous model, where runs are admissible in $\mathcal{M}^{\text{ASYNC}}$ and processes can query failure detector $\mathcal{D}$ in any step, as $\langle \mathcal{M}^{\text{ASYNC}}, \mathcal{D} \rangle$.

Definition 7.2.1. If there is an algorithm A that solves problem P in $\langle \mathcal{M}^{\text{ASYNC}}, \mathcal{D} \rangle$, we say that $\mathcal{D}$ *solves* P.

We say that algorithm $A_{\mathcal{D} \to \mathcal{D}'}$ transforms $\mathcal{D}$ to $\mathcal{D}'$, if processes maintain output variables $output_{\mathcal{D}'}$ that emulate failure detector histories of $\mathcal{D}'$ that are admissible for F. Based on this notion of transforming oracles, Chandra and Toueg (1996) have introduced a comparison relation on failure detectors:

Definition 7.2.2. We say that $\mathcal{D}'$ is *weaker* than $\mathcal{D}$ and call $\mathcal{D}$ *stronger* than $\mathcal{D}'$, if such an algorithm $A_{\mathcal{D} \to \mathcal{D}'}$ exist. If there is also an algorithm $A_{\mathcal{D}' \to \mathcal{D}}$, we say that $\mathcal{D}$ and $\mathcal{D}'$ are *equivalent*. If no such algorithm $A_{\mathcal{D}' \to \mathcal{D}}$ exists, we say that $\mathcal{D}$ is *strictly stronger* than $\mathcal{D}'$; *strictly weaker* is defined analogously. If neither $A_{\mathcal{D} \to \mathcal{D}'}$ nor $A_{\mathcal{D}' \to \mathcal{D}}$ exists then we say that $\mathcal{D}$ and $\mathcal{D}'$ are *incomparable*. A failure detector $\mathcal{D}'$ is the *weakest for problem* P if $\mathcal{D}$ is weaker than any failure detector $\mathcal{D}$ that solves P.

Chapter 7. The Generalized Loneliness Detector $\mathcal{L}(k)$

Recently, it was shown by Delporte-Gallet et al. (2008) that the "loneliness"-detector $\mathcal{L}$ is the weakest failure detector for message passing $(n-1)$-set agreement. Intuitively speaking, there is one (not necessarily correct!) process where $\mathcal{L}$ perpetually outputs FALSE, and, if all except one process p have crashed, $\mathcal{L}$ eventually outputs TRUE at p forever.

We now present a natural generalization of $\mathcal{L}$ that will turn out to be sufficient for k-set agreement.

Definition 7.2.3. The $(n{-}k)$-loneliness detector $\mathcal{L}(k)$ outputs either TRUE or FALSE, such that for all environments $\mathcal{E}$ and $\forall F \in \mathcal{E}$ it holds that there is a set of processes $\Pi_0 \subseteq \Pi$, $|\Pi_0| = n - k$ and a correct process $q \notin \Pi_0$ such that:

$$\forall p \in \Pi_0 \ \forall t\colon H(p,t) = \text{FALSE} \tag{7.1}$$

$$|F| \geqslant k \implies \exists t \ \forall t' \geqslant t\colon H(q,t') = \text{TRUE} \tag{7.2}$$

7.3. Tightness of $\mathcal{L}(k)$

To show that $\mathcal{L}(k)$ tightly encapsulates the necessary amount of solvability power for k-set agreement, we will first prove that $\mathcal{L}(k)$ does *not* provide much stronger properties than needed, by showing that $(k{-}1)$-set agreement is impossible.

Theorem 7.3.1

> Let k be such that $2 \leqslant k \leqslant n-1$. There is no algorithm that solves $(k{-}1)$-set agreement in the model $\langle \mathcal{M}^{ASYNC}, \mathcal{L}(k) \rangle$.

Proof. We assume by contradiction that such an algorithm A exists. Now consider the failure detector history where $\mathcal{L}$ outputs TRUE at processes $p_1, \ldots, p_k$, while it outputs FALSE at the other processes. Formally speaking, this means the following:

$$\forall t\colon H(p_i, t) = \begin{cases} \text{TRUE} & \text{if } 1 \leqslant i \leqslant k; \\ \text{FALSE} & \text{otherwise} \end{cases}$$

Clearly, this defines a legal history for $\mathcal{L}(k)$ in a run where the $n-k$ processes

$$p_{k+1}, \ldots, p_n$$

crash initially. For the remaining k processes, the failure detector provides no (further) information about failures, as it outputs TRUE perpetually. Since A is able to solve $(k-1)$-set agreement in any such run by assumption, it can also be used to solve $(k-1)$-set agreement in an asynchronous system of k processes, equipped with a dummy failure detector (Guerraoui et al., 2007) that always outputs TRUE. This, however, contradicts the $(n-1)$-set agreement impossibility in a system of n processes (see Saks and Zaharoglou, 2000; Borowsky and Gafni, 1993; Herlihy and Shavit, 1993). □

7.4. Solving k-Set Agreement with $\mathcal{L}(k)$

In this section, we present an algorithm that solves k-set agreement in the asynchronous model augmented with $\mathcal{L}(k)$. The original algorithm for solving $(n-1)$-set agreement with $\mathcal{L}$ (see Delporte-Gallet et al., 2008) requires a total order on process identifiers. Algorithm 5, in contrast, also works in anonymous systems.[2] We therefore consider the variant of model $\mathcal{M}^{\text{ASYNC}}$ where process identifiers are indistinguishable by the algorithm. Note carefully that this means that processes do *not* know the sender of a received message. Clearly, point-to-point communication does not make sense in this setting; we assume that processes have access to broadcast communication

Overview of the Algorithm

Algorithm 5 proceeds in asynchronous rounds. In every round r, every process p that has not yet decided, queries its failure detector and decides if $\mathcal{L}(k)$ outputs TRUE. Otherwise, p checks if it has received $n-k+1$ round r messages; note that this check is non-blocking. If so, p updates its current estimate x to the minimum of these messages.

At a first glance, it might appear to be counterintuitive that processes terminate after $k+2$ rounds. After all, it would be reasonable to expect that harder agreement tasks like consensus require *more* rounds than, for example, $(n-1)$-set agreement. The reason why this is not the case here is that $\mathcal{L}(k)$ itself becomes much weaker for values of k close to $n-1$, since there are less processes that perpetually output false. To see why $k+2$ rounds are necessary, suppose that the process, which has currently the largest decision estimate, decides in Line 10 after sending its round $r(=0)$ message. We will show below (see Lemma 7.4.2) that the number of distinct values of x in the system is at most k after the remaining processes have received $n-k+1$ round messages and executed Line 18. Thus, we might end up with $k+1$ distinct decision values if these processes do not continue to round $r+1$. Then, again the process having the largest

---
[2] Note that Algorithm 5 does require knowledge of n, i.e., of the total number of processes in the system.

Algorithm 5 Solving k-set agreement with $\mathcal{L}(k)$

Variables:
1: $v \in \mathbb{N}$ // the input value
2: $x \in \mathbb{N}$ // the estimated decision value
3: $rnd \in \mathbb{N}$
Initially:
4: $x \leftarrow v$
5: $rnd \leftarrow 0$
6: broadcast $(round, 0, x)$

In any later step:
7: receive messages
8: **if** $\mathcal{L}(k) = $ TRUE **then**
9:     broadcast (dec, x)
10:    decide x
11:    halt
12: **else if** received (dec, y) **then**
13:    broadcast (dec, y)
14:    decide y
15:    halt
16: **else if** received $\geqslant n - k + 1$ $(round, rnd, y)$ messages **then**
17:    $S \leftarrow \{y_1, \ldots, y_{n-k+1}\}$
18:    $x \leftarrow \min(S)$
19:    **if** $rnd = k + 1$ **then**
20:        broadcast (dec, x)
21:        decide x
22:        halt
23:    $rnd \leftarrow rnd + 1$
24:    broadcast $(round, r, x)$

value could decide in Line 10 after having sent its round $r + 1$ message and the same argument applies. At the end of round $k + 1$ every process that has not yet decided, decides on its current estimate. As we will show below, this decision is safe, due to the fact that $\mathcal{L}(k)$ outputs TRUE at no more than k processes.

Proof of Correctness

For the purpose of our correctness proof, we denote by X^r the possibly empty array containing the (not necessarily distinct) x-values of all alive processes in the system after the assignment in line 18 when $rnd = r$. We assume that X^r is ordered by decreasing values, i.e., $X^r[1]$ is the maximal value, if it exists. Furthermore, we denote the support of X^r, i.e., the number of nonempty entries in X^r by $|X^r|$, and the number of unique values among those by u^r. We immediately have the following fact:

Observation 7.4.1. *For all rounds r, it holds that*

$$|X^r| \leqslant n - a^r,$$

where a^r is the number of processes which never sent their respective $(round, r, x)$ message.

Lemma 7.4.2. *For any round $r \geqslant 1$, the number of unique values in X^r is*

$$u^r \leqslant k - a^r.$$

Proof. First, we observe that x is updated by a process p only after receiving $n - k + 1$ round r messages. Let p be the process that assigns the largest value in Line 18. Since any process p sets x to the minimum of the $n - k + 1$ round r values received, there must be $n - k + 1$ messages containing values $y_1, \ldots, y_{n-k+1} \geqslant x$ among those received by p.

By Observation 7.4.1, it follows that only

$$n - a^r - (n - k + 1) = k - a^r - 1$$

values in X^r can be smaller than p's minimum. Thus, processes assign at most $k - a^r$ different values to x and subsequently send them as $(round, r + 1, x)$-messages. $\square$

Lemma 7.4.3. *Processes do not decide on more than k different values.*

Proof. Regarding the number of different decision values, processes deciding due to receiving a (dec, y) message (line 14) make no difference, since some other process must have decided on y using another method before. Thus we can ignore this case here.

What remains are decisions due to $\mathcal{L}(k)$ being TRUE (line 10) and due to having received $n - k + 1$ messages in round $k + 1$ (line 21). For each $r \geqslant 0$, we denote by ℓ_r the number of processes which have decided due to their failure detector output being TRUE while their $rnd = r$. Thus the number of processes that have decided in line 10 with $rnd \leqslant r$ for some $r \geqslant 0$ is $\Sigma_{s=0}^{r} \ell_s$. In the following we use Σ^r as an abbreviation for this sum. Since processes halt after deciding, we can deduce that the number of processes

which do not send round r messages a_r, is at least Σ^{r-1}. Thus, Lemma 7.4.2 tells us that
$$u_r \leqslant k - \Sigma^{r-1}.$$
Now assume by contradiction that there are actually $D > k$ decisions, with $D = u_{k+1} + \Sigma^{k+1}$, that is the number of different values decided on in line 21 plus those that decided based on $\mathcal{L}(k)$. Thus we get
$$u_{k+1} > k - \Sigma^{k+1},$$
and by using the above property of u_r, we deduce that $\Sigma^{k+1} > \Sigma^k$, and thus $\ell_{k+1} \geqslant 1$. These processes must have decided on some values in X^k, however, which implies $D = u_k + \Sigma^k$, as obviously $x \in X^{k+1} \Rightarrow x \in X^k$. We can repeat this argument until we reach
$$D = u_1 + \Sigma^0 = u_1 + \ell_0.$$
Here, Lemma 7.4.2 gives us the trivial upper bound $u_1 \leqslant k$, which entails the requirement $\ell_0 \geqslant 1$ as $D > k$.

By now, we have shown that, assuming $D > k$ decisions $\ell_r \geqslant 1$ for $r \in \{0, \ldots, k+1\}$. In other words we have deduced that
$$\Sigma^{k+1} \geqslant k+1$$
processes have decided due to their $\mathcal{L}(k)$ output being TRUE. This contradicts property (7.2) of $\mathcal{L}(k)$, thus proving Lemma 9.3.15. □

Theorem 7.4.4

Algorithm 5 solves k-set agreement in the anonymous asynchronous system augmented with $\mathcal{L}(k)$, where up to $n-1$ processes can fail by crashing.

Proof. *Validity* is evident, since no value other than the initial values v of processes are ever assigned directly or indirectly to x. *k-Agreement* follows from Lemma 7.4.3, and since either $n - k$ processes send messages in each round or some process has $\mathcal{L}(k) = $ TRUE, every correct process *terminates*. □

From Delporte-Gallet et al. (2008), we know that $\mathcal{L}$ can be extracted anonymously from any failure detector D which solves set agreement using some algorithm A: Every process executes an independent instance of A (without any other process participating) using D as failure detector. The simulated $\mathcal{L}$ outputs TRUE at p only after A has terminated at p. In conjunction with Theorem 7.4.4, this implies the following fact:

Corollary 7.4.5. $\mathcal{L}$ *is the weakest failure detector for set agreement in anonymous message passing systems.*

7.5. Relation between $\mathcal{L}(k)$ and $\mathcal{S}_{n-k+1}$

In the remainder of this chapter, we will analyse how the $\mathcal{L}(k)$ failure detector relates to existing failure detectors for k-set agreement.

In this section we will analyze the relationship between $\mathcal{L}(k)$ and failure detector $\mathcal{S}_{n-k+1}$. The strong failure detector $\mathcal{S}$ (see Chandra and Toueg, 1996) outputs sets of process ids, a so called suspect list, and ensures that some correct process is never (falsely) suspected, a property which is called *weak accuracy*. Moreover, the *strong completeness* property of $\mathcal{S}$ guarantees that eventually all faulty processes are suspected. As shown by Chandra and Toueg (1996), $\mathcal{S}$ is sufficient for solving consensus.

The limited scope failure detectors of Mostéfaoui and Raynal (1999b) and Guerraoui and Schiper (1996) have the strong completeness property (see condition (7.4) below) of $\mathcal{S}$, but their accuracy property is limited to a set of processes called the *scope* (see (7.3)). In the special case where the scope comprises all processes, $\mathcal{S}_n$ coincides with $\mathcal{S}$. It was shown by Mostéfaoui and Raynal (2000) that $\mathcal{S}_{n-k+1}$ is sufficient for k-set agreement in a wait-free environment.

Definition 7.5.1. The *strong failure detector with x-limited scope* is denoted by $\mathcal{S}_x$ and is defined such that for all environments $\mathcal{E}$ and $\forall F \in \mathcal{E}$, there is a set $Q \subseteq \Pi : |Q| = x$ such that:

$$\exists p \in (Q \setminus F) \; \forall t \; \forall q \in Q: \; p \notin H(q, t) \quad (7.3)$$
$$\forall p \in F \; \exists t \; \forall t' \geqslant t \forall q \in \Pi: \; p \in H(q, t') \quad (7.4)$$

In Theorem 7.5.5 we will show that, except in the canonical cases $k = 1$ and $k = n - 1$, failure detectors $\mathcal{S}_{n-k+1}$ and $\mathcal{L}(k)$ are incomparable. We will start out with some technical lemmas:

Lemma 7.5.2. $\mathcal{L}(1)$ *is stronger than* $\mathcal{S}_n = \mathcal{S}$.

Proof. In order to show that $\mathcal{L}(1)$ is stronger than $\mathcal{S}_n$, we show that we can implement $\mathcal{S}_n$ with $\mathcal{L}(1)$. For $\mathcal{S}$, we have to find one correct process which is never suspected by anyone (weak accuracy), while eventually every faulty process is suspected (strong completeness). As $\mathcal{L}(1)$ must output TRUE at one correct process only if at least one process has crashed, the idea of the transformation is quite simple: A process always outputs the empty set as its suspicion list, unless (1) it is instructed otherwise by another process, or (2) its $\mathcal{L}(1)$ outputs TRUE. Since $n-1$ processes must output FALSE, case (2) can only occur at a single process p, which then sends a message to all other processes telling them to suspect everyone but p.

Strong completeness follows, because if one (or more) processes crash, $\mathcal{L}(1)$ will eventually output TRUE at some correct p, causing all faulty processes to be suspected (along with all correct processes apart from p) by all other processes. Weak accuracy follows from p never being suspected. □

Next we consider the general case, i.e., $1 < k < n$. We will show that, for any such k, $\mathcal{L}(k)$ is not stronger than even the weakest (non-trivial) instance of $\mathcal{S}_x$, namely $\mathcal{S}_2$.

Lemma 7.5.3. *Failure detector $\mathcal{L}(k)$ is not stronger than $\mathcal{S}_2$, for all $k > 1$.*

Proof. Assume in contradiction that a transformation T exists, which implements $\mathcal{S}_2$ based on $\mathcal{L}(k)$. Now consider a run α where only p crashes initially, i.e., $|F| = 1$. Since

$$|F| \leqslant 1 < k,$$

$\mathcal{L}(k)$ can perpetually output FALSE at all processes in α. By the *strong completeness* property of $\mathcal{S}_2$, transformation T must ensure that there is some time t such that all processes suspect p.

Now consider a different run α' where all messages from p to other processes are delayed until $t' > t$. Moreover, assume that all processes except p crash at some time $t'' > t'$ in α' and consider the failure detector history H where $\mathcal{L}(k)$ outputs TRUE at p, and FALSE at all processes $q \neq p$. Clearly H is a valid history for α' and p has to be in the output suspect-list of all processes $q \neq p$ by time t, as α' is indistinguishable until t' from α. But since in α' all processes except p crash at time t'', p is the only correct process, but was suspected by all other processes, contradicting 2-weak accuracy (7.3). □

For the converse case, we show that no reduction from $\mathcal{S}_{n-k+1}$ to $\mathcal{L}(k)$ exists.

Lemma 7.5.4. *$\mathcal{S}_{n-k+1}$ is not stronger than $\mathcal{L}(k)$, for $k < n - 1$.*

Proof. We again assume by contradiction that a suitable transformation algorithm T exists, which builds $\mathcal{L}(k)$ from $\mathcal{S}_{n-k+1}$. Let α_i be the run where all processes except p_i crash initially. Moreover, suppose that p_i suspects every other process throughout the entire execution. Then, as p_i is the only remaining correct process, it must eventually set $output_{\mathcal{L}(k)}$ to TRUE at some time t_i. By applying this construction to a set

$$S = \{p_1, \ldots, p_{k-1}\}$$

of processes, we get a time

$$t = \max\{t_1, \ldots, t_{k-1}\},$$

when every p_i has set $output_{\mathcal{L}(k)}$ to TRUE in the respective α_i.

Now consider a run α where every process in the set S perpetually suspects every other process, that is

$$\forall t\ \forall p_i \in S \colon H(p_i, t) = \Pi \setminus \{p_i\},$$

process p_k never suspects anyone, and every process in $\Pi \setminus S \cup \{p_k\}$ does not suspect p_k. Setting

$$x = n - k + 1,$$
$$\Pi \setminus Q = S,$$
$$p = p_k \in Q, \text{ and}$$
$$q \in Q \setminus \{p_k\}$$

in Definition 7.5.1 reveals that this does not violate $(n-k+1)$-weak accuracy of $\mathcal{S}_{n-k+1}$. Moreover, in run α, the delivery of all messages from all processes to any process in S is delayed until time t.

Then, for any process $p_i \in S$, the run α is indistinguishable from the run α_i where only p_i is alive and so all $k-1$ processes in S have set $output_{\mathcal{L}(k)}$ to TRUE by time t in α. Now suppose that all processes in S crash at some time $t' > t$, and also assume that p_k initially crashes.

Since k processes crash in α, it follows by the fact that T implements $\mathcal{L}(k)$ that at least one of the remaining processes

$$p_{k+1}, p_{k+2}, \ldots, p_n$$

has to set $output_{\mathcal{L}(k)}$ to TRUE eventually. Without loss of generality, let p_{k+1} be that process and let t_{k+1} be the time when it does so. Since $n \geqslant k+2$, we can assume that p_{k+1} crashes after t_{k+1} as well, and repeat the argument for process p_{k+2}. But then

$k+1$ processes have set their output variable $output_{\mathcal{L}(k)}$ to TRUE, which contradicts the requirement (7.1) of $\mathcal{L}(k)$. □

We are now ready to state the following theorem:

Theorem 7.5.5
Failure detector $\mathcal{S}_n$ is strictly weaker than $\mathcal{L}(1)$, and $\mathcal{S}_2$ is strictly stronger than failure detector $\mathcal{L}(n-1)$. For $1 < k < n-1$, $\mathcal{L}(1)$ and $\mathcal{S}_{n-k+1}$ are incomparable.

Proof. From Lemma 7.5.2 and 7.5.4 it follows that $\mathcal{S}_n$ is strictly weaker than $\mathcal{L}(1)$. Moreover, Lemma 7.5.3 and the result that $\mathcal{L} = \mathcal{L}(n-1)$ is the weakest failure detector for set agreement (Delporte-Gallet et al., 2008) implies that $\mathcal{S}_2$ is strictly stronger than $\mathcal{L}(n-1)$. For the remaining choices of k, we get that $\mathcal{S}_{n-k+1}$ and $\mathcal{L}(k)$ are not comparable by Lemma 7.5.4 and 7.5.3, which completes the proof. □

Recalling the result of Jayanti and Toueg (2008), namely that every problem has a weakest failure detector, Theorem 7.5.5 immediately implies:

Corollary 7.5.6. *Neither $\mathcal{L}(k)$ nor $\mathcal{S}_{n-k+1}$ is the weakest failure detector for general message passing k-set agreement.*

Despite this somewhat negative result, $\mathcal{L}(k)$ appears to be a promising candidate for a weakest failure detector for message passing k-set agreement in anonymous systems, as we will discuss in the following section.

7.6. Relation between $\mathcal{L}(k)$ and Σ_k

We now explore the relationship between $\mathcal{L}(k)$ and the generalized quorum detector of Bonnet and Raynal (2009). While the weakest failure detector for message passing k-set agreement is still unknown, the *quorum family* Σ_k was shown to be necessary for solving k-set agreement with any failure detector $\mathcal{X}$, in the sense that there is a transformation that implements Σ_k in the system $\langle \mathcal{M}^{\text{ASYNC}}, \mathcal{X} \rangle$.

Definition 7.6.1 (Bonnet and Raynal (2009))**.** The *generalized quorum failure detector* Σ_k, with $\Sigma = \Sigma_1$, outputs a set of trusted process ids, such that for all environments $\mathcal{E}$ and for all failure patterns $F \in \mathcal{E}$ the following holds:

Intersection: For every set of $k+1$ processes $\{p_1, \ldots, p_{k+1}\}$ and for all $k+1$ time instants $t_1, \ldots, t_{k+1}$, there exist indices i and j with $1 \leqslant i \neq j \leqslant k+1$, such that

$$H(p_i, t_i) \cap H(p_j, t_j) \neq \emptyset.$$

Liveness: $\exists t \; \forall t' \geqslant t \; \forall p_i \notin F \colon H(p_i, t') \cap F = \emptyset.$

If a process p crashes at time t, i.e., $p \in F(t)$, we define that

$$\forall t' \geqslant t \colon H(p, t') = \Pi.$$

We will first consider the standard quorum failure detector $\Sigma = \Sigma_1$. The following result is obtained by generalizing the result of Delporte-Gallet et al. (2008, Lemma 4) by finding a suitable partitioning.

Theorem 7.6.2

$\mathcal{L}(k)$ *is not stronger than* Σ, *if* $n > 2$ *and* $k \geqslant 2$.

Proof. Assume that there exists an algorithm A that transforms $\mathcal{L}(k)$ (for some $k \geqslant 2$) into Σ. Consider the partitioning of Π given by

$$P = \{\{p_1\}, \{p_2\}, P_3\}.$$

Since

$$n - 1 \geqslant k \geqslant 2,$$

this is a valid partitioning. Moreover, assume two runs r_1 and r_2 such that process p_i is correct in run r_i and all other processes are faulty from the beginning. Moreover, let the output of $\mathcal{L}(k)$ at process p_i be TRUE from the beginning as well; note that the output at all other processes is FALSE by definition. Since A must guarantee liveness for Σ, it eventually has to output $\{p_i\}$ in run r_i, say, at time t_i. Now imagine a run r in which the processes p_1 and p_2 are correct, the output of $\mathcal{L}(k)$ is TRUE from the beginning, and

$\mathcal{L}(k)$ outputs FALSE at processes in P_3. Additionally, no message of a process from a different partition is received by these two processes before time

$$t = \max\{t_1, t_2\}.$$

Then, runs r_1 and r_2 are indistinguishable from run r before time t. Therefore, the output of Σ at p_i at time t_i will be the same as in r_i. But this contradicts the intersection property of Σ. So there exists no such algorithm A. □

When considering the generalized quorum failure detector Σ_k, we know by Bonnet and Raynal (2009, 2010b) that Σ_k is necessary for solving k-set agreement, hence, Σ_k is weaker than $\mathcal{L}(k)$, for all $1 \leqslant k \leqslant n-1$. Note, however, that it is unknown whether there is an algorithm for solving k-set agreement with Σ_k. The following theorem shows that Σ_k is strictly weaker than $\mathcal{L}(k)$, for any $k < n - 1$.

Theorem 7.6.3

Let $k < n - 1$. Failure detector Σ_k is strictly weaker than $\mathcal{L}(k)$.

Proof. The proof is similar to the proof of Lemma 7.5.4. We assume in contradiction that there is a suitable transformation algorithm T that implements $\mathcal{L}(k)$ in the system $\langle \mathcal{M}^{\text{ASYNC}}, \Sigma_k \rangle$.

Let α_i be a run where all processes except p_i crash initially and assume that

$$\forall t' \colon H(p_i, t') = \{p_i\}.$$

Then, as p_i is the only remaining correct process, it must eventually set $output_{\mathcal{L}(k)}$ to TRUE at some time t_i. By applying this construction to a set of processes

$$S = \{p_1, \ldots, p_{k-1}\},$$

we get a time

$$t = \max\{t_1, \ldots, t_{k-1}\},$$

when every p_i has set $output_{\mathcal{L}(k)}$ to TRUE in the respective α_i.

Now consider a run α where, just like in α_i, every process in S trusts no other process until time t, i.e.,

$$\forall t' \leqslant t \; \forall p_i \in S \colon H(p_i, t') = \{p_i\},$$

and suppose that process p_k crashes initially:

$$\forall t'\colon H(p_k, t') = \Pi. \tag{7.5}$$

For any process $p_\ell \notin S \cup \{p_k\}$, we assume that

$$\forall t'\colon H(p_\ell, t') = \Pi \setminus F. \tag{7.6}$$

Moreover, let the run α be such that the delivery of all messages from other processes to any process in S is delayed until time t.

Clearly, for any process $p_i \in S$, the run α is indistinguishable from the run α_i where only p_i is alive and so all $k-1$ processes in S have set $output_{\mathcal{L}(k)}$ to TRUE by time t in α. Assume that all processes in S crash at time $t+1$ in α.

Since k processes crash in α and due to the assumption that the transformation T implements $\mathcal{L}(k)$ it follows that at least one of the remaining processes

$$p_{k+1}, p_{k+2}, \ldots, p_n$$

has to set $output_{\mathcal{L}(k)}$ to TRUE eventually; w.l.o.g. let p_{k+1} be that process and let t_{k+1} be the time when it does so. However, since $n \geqslant k+2$, we can assume that p_{k+1} crashes in α at $t_{k+1} + 1$, and repeat the argument for process p_{k+2}; again, assume that p_{k+2} sets $output_{\mathcal{L}(k)}$ to TRUE at time t_{k+2} and then crashes at $t_{k+2} + 1$. We have therefore constructed α such that, by time

$$\max\{t, t_{k+1}, t_{k+2}\},$$

$k+1$ processes have set their output variable $output_{\mathcal{L}(k)}$ to TRUE, which contradicts the requirement (7.1) of $\mathcal{L}(k)$.

What remains to be shown is that the failure detector histories of the constructed run α satisfy the definition of Σ_k (see Definition 7.6.1). First, observe that (7.6) implies the liveness condition of Σ_k, since all correct processes are in $\Pi \setminus S$. For the intersection property, consider any set M of $k+1$ processes. Since $|S| = k-1$, at least two processes $p_j, p'_j \in M$ are in $\Pi \setminus S$. Then, (7.5) and (7.6) guarantee that the corresponding histories $H(p_j, t_1)$ and $H(p'_j, t_2)$ intersect for any two points in time t_1 and t_2, which completes the proof. □

7.7. $\mathcal{L}(k)$ in Anonymous Systems

In this section we will focus on systems where processes do not have unique identifiers. More specifically, throughout this section we assume a variant of the asynchronous model $\mathcal{M}^{\text{ASYNC}}$ where all process identifiers are identical and processes communicate via a broadcast primitive. Recall from Chapter 7 that Algorithm 5 (on Page 96) achieves k-set agreement in this setting when processes have access to $\mathcal{L}(k)$.

Recently, Bonnet and Raynal (2010a) have presented an in-depth analysis of various failure detectors for solving consensus (i.e. 1-set agreement) in such anonymous systems. We will now restate the properties of some of these failure detectors:

Definition 7.7.1 (Bonnet and Raynal (2010a)). The *identity-free perfect failure detector* AP provides processes with an integer variable *acnp* such that the following hold:
(1) *acnp* is never greater than the number of crashed processes.
(2) Eventually *acnp* is exactly equal to the number of crashed processes.

Intuitively speaking, variable *acnp* provides an (eventually tight) lower bound on the number of crashes.

Definition 7.7.2 (Bonnet and Raynal (2010a)). The *identity-free eventual leader oracle* $A\Omega$ provides a boolean value *a_leader* at each process, such that
(1) eventually *a_leader* is forever TRUE at exactly 1 correct process p_i, and
(2) eventually *a_leader* is forever FALSE for all processes $\neq p_i$.

Bonnet and Raynal (2010a) also introduce an anonymous counterpart of the quorum failure detector Σ; as we will not use this failure detector $A\Sigma$ directly, we omit the formal definition here.

Furthermore, Bonnet and Raynal (2010a) conjecture that $(A\Sigma, A\Omega) \oplus AP$ is the weakest failure detector for solving anonymous consensus. This $\oplus$-*combination* is defined as the failure detector that outputs $\bot$ for an arbitrary finite prefix and then chooses an output that is admissible for *either* $(A\Sigma, A\Omega)$ or AP at every process. Note that this choice is completely independent of the failure pattern of the run.

In the remainder of this chapter we will disprove this conjecture by showing that $(A\Sigma, A\Omega) \oplus AP$ cannot be extracted from $\mathcal{L}(1)$.

Lemma 7.7.3. *Failure detector $\mathcal{L}(1)$ is not stronger than $(A\Sigma, A\Omega) \oplus AP$, in an anonymous system of at least 2 processes.*

Proof. We assume in contradiction that there is some extraction algorithm T that implements $(A\Sigma, A\Omega) \oplus AP$ on top of $\mathcal{L}(k)$.

Consider a run α where no process crashes, processes perform steps synchronously and $\mathcal{L}(1)$ outputs FALSE at every process forever. Since we have assumed an anonymous system, it suffices to notice that processes do not have a way of eventually breaking this symmetry, which is required for satisfying the properties of $A\Omega$ (Definition 7.7.2). Therefore, the extraction algorithm T must eventually output a history that is admissible for AP in α, from some time t on. (Before time t, algorithm T outputs $\perp$ at every process.)

Now consider a run β that is identical to α up to time t and where some process p_1 crashes at time $t + 1$. The history of $\mathcal{L}(1)$ (see Definition 7.2.3 on Page 94) in β is such that it will output TRUE at time $t_{\text{true}} > t$ at some correct process; without loss of generality, let p_2 be that process. Definition 7.7.1 requires the set of remaining correct processes

$$S = \{p_2, \ldots, p_n\}$$

to eventually set their simulated output variable

$$acnp = 1.$$

Let t_{acnp} be the time when the first process $p_i \in S$ does so; note that $t_{acnp} \geq t+1$, by Definition 7.7.1.(1). Now consider a run γ that is otherwise identical to β, but where all messages sent by p_1 are delayed until after time t_{acnp}, and where $\mathcal{L}(1)$ outputs TRUE (only) at process p_2 at time t_{true}. Note that this is still a valid history for $\mathcal{L}(1)$. Moreover, all processes in S perform the exact same steps at the same time in both runs until time t_{acnp}. Clearly, γ is indistinguishable for all processes in S from run β until time t_{acnp}, and hence $p_i \in S$ must also set $acnp = 1$ at time t_{acnp} in γ. Considering that $acnp$ is an *over*-approximation of the number of crashed processes in γ, we have a contradiction to Definition 7.7.1. □

Lemma 7.7.4. *Failure detector* $(A\Sigma, A\Omega) \oplus AP$ *is not stronger than* $\mathcal{L}(1)$ *in an anonymous system of at least 3 processes.*

Proof. Since any failure detector history of AP is also a valid history for $(A\Sigma, A\Omega) \oplus AP$, it will be sufficient to show that $\mathcal{L}(1)$ cannot be built from AP. Therefore, assume in contradiction that such a transformation algorithm exists. Consider a run α where some process p_1 crashes initially. In order to satisfy the properties of $\mathcal{L}(1)$, some correct process p_2 must eventually set its simulated output variable of $\mathcal{L}(1)$ to TRUE at some time t. Note that failure detector AP does not provide p_2 with any information on whether it will crash in the run or not. Furthermore, recall that $\mathcal{L}(1)$ outputs FALSE at $n-1$ processes perpetually. Thus, if p_2 crashes at time $t+1$, none of the remaining processes can set its output to TRUE without violating the perpetual property of $\mathcal{L}(1)$. □

Theorem 7.7.5
Consider an anonymous asynchronous system of at least 3 processes. Failure detectors $(A\Sigma, A\Omega) \oplus AP$ and $\mathcal{L}(1)$ are incomparable.

Proof. Follows immediately from Lemmas 7.7.3 and 7.7.4. □

Corollary 7.7.6. Neither $(A\Sigma, A\Omega) \oplus AP$ nor $\mathcal{L}(1)$ is a weakest failure detector for solving consensus in an anonymous asynchronous system.

7.8. Discussion

In this chapter we have introduced the generalized loneliness detector $\mathcal{L}(k)$ and showed how it can be used to solve k-set agreement. In fact, Algorithm 5 revealed that $\mathcal{L}(k)$ provides enough information for solving k-set agreement even in anonymous systems without unique process identifiers, which implies that $\mathcal{L}(n-1)$ is the weakest failure detector for $(n-1)$-set agreement in this setting.

Recall that $\mathcal{L}(n-1)$ coincides with $\mathcal{L}$, which is implementable in our models $\mathcal{M}^{\text{anti}}$ and $\mathcal{M}^{\text{sink}}$ (see Chapter 6). In the context of Figure 1.2 on Page 21, we must therefore place the model $\langle \mathcal{M}^{\text{ASYNC}}, \mathcal{L}(k) \rangle$ just above $\mathcal{M}^{\text{anti}}$ and $\mathcal{M}^{\text{sink}}$ and below the ABC model of Chapter 3.

We have also presented several relations between $\mathcal{L}(k)$ and existing failure detectors. While we have proved that $\mathcal{L}(k)$ cannot be the weakest one in non-anonymous systems, it surpasses existing failure detectors for k-set agreement in the aspect of not requiring processes to have unique ids, i.e., $\mathcal{L}(k)$ also works in anonymous systems, as we have shown in Theorem 7.4.4.

Considering the incomparability of $\mathcal{L}(k)$ and $\mathcal{S}_{n-k+1}$ for $1 < k < n-1$, the combined failure detector $\mathcal{L}(k) \oplus \mathcal{S}_{n-k+1}$ might be a promising candidate for the weakest failure detector for these cases. It is trivial to show that $\mathcal{L}(k) \oplus \mathcal{S}_{n-k+1}$ can solve k-set agreement by simply ignoring the finite prefix where the failure detector outputs $\bot$, and then using one of the existing algorithms for $\mathcal{L}(k)$ or $\mathcal{S}_{n-k+1}$, as needed. Moreover, it is also obvious that this detector is weaker than $\mathcal{L}(k)$ and $\mathcal{S}_{n-k+1}$, as any history that is admissible for

$\mathcal{L}(k)$ or $\mathcal{S}_{n-k+1}$ is also admissible for $\mathcal{L}(k) \oplus \mathcal{S}_{n-k+1}$. Further investigation of $\mathcal{L}(k) \oplus \mathcal{S}_{n-k+1}$ is part of our future research.

Another interesting research direction is the quest for the weakest failure detector in anonymous systems. The results of Section 7.7 show that finding a suitable candidate failure detector in the anonymous setting is a difficult task, due to the inherent incomparability of different anonymous failure detectors and the inability to specify suitable extraction algorithms without referring to process identifiers. Nevertheless, the combined detector $(A\Sigma, A\Omega) \oplus AP \oplus \mathcal{L}(1)$ appears to be worth pursuing.

Chapter 8

On the Impossibility of k-Set Agreement

> A likely impossibility is always preferable to an unconvincing possibility.
>
> *(Aristotle)*

IN THIS CHAPTER we will present a theorem[1] that provides us with a generic mechanism for proving the impossibility of achieving k-set agreement in different system models. Unlike previous impossibility results for shared-memory systems (see Borowsky and Gafni, 1993; Herlihy and Shavit, 1993; Saks and Zaharoglou, 2000), Theorem 8.2.1 is much more straightforward: Instead of using algebraic topology or a variant of Sperner's Lemma, our result employs a reduction to the impossibility of achieving consensus in a certain subsystem.

We have employed a similar reduction technique in the proofs of Theorem 6.2.1 (Page 89) and Theorem 7.3.1 (Page 94), where we showed that consensus is impossible in models $\mathcal{M}^{\text{anti}}$ and $\mathcal{M}^{\text{sink}}$. Bouzid and Travers (2010) have also used a similar reduction argument.

---

[1] The results of this chapter are joint work with Martin Biely and Ulrich Schmid.

Restrictions of Algorithms and Indistinguishability of Runs

Throughout this chapter we basically assume the model $\mathcal{M}^{\mathrm{ASYNC}}$. For the concrete instantiations of our theorem in Section 8.3, we will sometimes assume that $\mathcal{M}^{\mathrm{ASYNC}}$ is augmented with a failure detector (see Section 7.2), or strengthen the model by assuming (partially) synchronous processes, as we did for model $\mathcal{M}^{\mathrm{sink}}$ in Chapter 6.

In the previous chapters of this thesis we always assumed some system model $\mathcal{M}$ and a fixed set of processes Π running in $\mathcal{M}$. In this chapter we will occasionally use a subsystem $\mathcal{M}'$ that is a *restriction* of $\mathcal{M}$, in the sense that it consists of a subset of processes in Π, while using the same mode of computation (atomicity of computing steps, time-driven vs. message-driven, etc.) as $\mathcal{M}$. We therefore use the notation

$$\mathcal{M} = \langle \Pi \rangle$$

and

$$\mathcal{M}' = \langle D \rangle,$$

for some set of processes $D \subseteq \Pi$.

Definition 8.0.1 (Restriction of an Algorithm). Let A be an algorithm that works in system $\mathcal{M} = \langle \Pi \rangle$ and let $D \subseteq \Pi$ be a nonempty set of processes. Consider a restricted system $\mathcal{M}' = \langle D \rangle$. The *restricted algorithm* $A_{|D}$ for system $\mathcal{M}'$ is constructed by dropping all messages sent to processes outside D in the message sending function of A, obtaining the message sending function of $A_{|D}$.

Note that we do not change the actual code of algorithm A in any way. In particular, the restricted algorithm still uses the value of $|\Pi|$ for the size of the system, even though the real size of D might be much smaller.

Whereas this is sufficient for running an algorithm designed for $\mathcal{M}$ in the restricted system $\mathcal{M}'$, in practice, one would also remove any dead code (resulting from state transitions triggered by message arrivals from processes in $\Pi \setminus D$, from the transition relation of A to obtain the actual transition relation of $A_{|D}$. Just like in Chapter 5, we use $\mathcal{M}_A$ to denote the set of runs of algorithm A in model $\mathcal{M}$.

We will use a concept of similarity/indistinguishability of runs that is slightly weaker than the usual notion (see Lynch, 1996, Page 21), as we require the same states only *until* a decision state is reached.[2] This makes a difference for algorithms where p can help others in reaching their decision after p has decided, for example, by forwarding messages.

Definition 8.0.2 (Indistinguishability of Runs). *Two runs α and β are indistinguishable (until decision) for a process p, if p has the same sequence of states in α and β until p decides. By*

$$\alpha \stackrel{D}{\sim} \beta$$

we denote the fact that α and β are indistinguishable for every $p \in D$.

Definition 8.0.3 (Compatibility of Runs). *Let $\mathcal{R}$ and $\mathcal{R}'$ be sets of runs. We say that runs $\mathcal{R}'$ are compatible with runs $\mathcal{R}$ for processes in D, denoted by $\mathcal{R}' \preceq_D \mathcal{R}$, if*

$$\forall \alpha \in \mathcal{R}'\ \exists \beta \in \mathcal{R}\colon \alpha \stackrel{D}{\sim} \beta.$$

8.1. T-Independence

We will now introduce a notion for message passing systems that is similar to the *progress conditions* of concurrent objects (see Taubenfeld, 2010; Imbs et al., 2010) in shared memory models.

Note that we consider algorithms for decision tasks, like for example k-set agreement. That is, every correct process must eventually decide.

Definition 8.1.1 (T-independence). *Consider a model $\mathcal{M} = \langle \Pi \rangle$ and some family of sets of processes $T \subseteq 2^\Pi$. We say that A satisfies T-independence in $\mathcal{M}$, if for all sets $D \in T$ it holds that in every run in $\mathcal{M}_A$ where the processes in D only receives messages from other processes in D, all processes in D either decide or crash.*

If p decides or crashes in every run in $\mathcal{M}_A$ where p eventually only receives messages from processes in D, we say that A satisfies eventual T-independence in $\mathcal{M}$.

Two observations are immediate:

Observation 8.1.2. *The following hold:*

(a) *Eventual T-independence implies T-independence.*

---
[2] Note that this notion of indistinguishability differs from the one used in Chapter 5, where we required all finite prefixes to be indistinguishable.

(b) If algorithm A satisfies T-independence in $\mathcal{M}$ and $T' \subseteq T$ then A satisfies T'-independence in $\mathcal{M}$.

We can express the following classic progress conditions in terms of T-independence: *Wait-freedom* (see Herlihy, 1991) corresponds exactly to eventual 2^Π-independence. Moreover, *obstruction-freedom* is implied by

$$\text{eventual } \{\{p_1\}, \ldots, \{p_n\}\}\text{-independence.}$$

The classic assumption of an *f-resilient* algorithm can be expressed by

$$\text{eventual } \{D \mid (D \subseteq \Pi) \wedge (|D| \geqslant |\Pi| - f)\}\text{-independence,}$$

whereas using (non-eventual) $\{D \mid (D \subseteq \Pi) \wedge (|D| \geqslant |\Pi| - f)\}$-independence is equivalent to tolerating up to f *initial crash failures*. Analogously to Imbs et al. (2010), T-independence also enables us to specify *asymmetric progress conditions*, e.g.,

$$\text{eventual } \{D \mid \{p_1\} \subseteq D \subseteq \Pi\}\text{-independence}$$

ensures wait-freedom for process p_1.

8.2. The Impossibility Theorem

In this section we will present our general k-set agreement impossibility theorem. Due to its very broad applicability, the theorem itself is stated in a highly generic way. The intuition behind this rather technical exposition will reveal itself in Section 8.3.

Theorem 8.2.1 (k-Set Agreement Impossibility)

Let $\mathcal{M} = \langle \Pi \rangle$ be a system model and consider the runs $\mathcal{M}_A$ that are generated by some fixed algorithm A in $\mathcal{M}$, where every process starts with a distinct input value. Fix some nonempty disjoint sets of processes $D_1, \ldots, D_{k-1}$, and a set of distinct decision values $\{v_1, \ldots, v_{k-1}\}$. Moreover, let $D = \bigcup_{1 \leqslant i < k} D_i$ and $\bar{D} = \Pi \setminus D$. Consider the following two properties:

(dec-D) For every set D_i, value v_i was proposed by some process in D, and every correct $p \in D_i$ decides on v_i.

(dec-$\bar{D}$) If $p_j \in \bar{D}$ then p_j receives no messages from any process in D until after p_j has decided.

> Let $\mathcal{R}_{(\bar{D})} \subseteq \mathcal{M}_A$ and $\mathcal{R}_{(D,\bar{D})} \subseteq \mathcal{M}_A$ be the sets of runs of A where (dec-$\bar{D}$) respectively (dec-D) and (dec-$\bar{D}$) hold.[3] Suppose that the following conditions hold:
>
> **(A)** Algorithm A satisfies $\{\bar{D}\}$-independence.
>
> **(B)** $\mathcal{R}_{(\bar{D})}$ is nonempty.
>
> **(C)** $\mathcal{R}_{(\bar{D})} \preceq_{\bar{D}} \mathcal{R}_{(D,\bar{D})}$.
>
> In addition, consider a restricted model $\mathcal{M}' = \langle \bar{D} \rangle$ such that the following hold:
>
> **(D)** There is no algorithm that solves consensus in $\mathcal{M}'$.
>
> **(E)** $\mathcal{M}'_{A|\bar{D}} \preceq_{\bar{D}} \mathcal{M}_A$.
>
> Then, A does not solve k-set agreement in $\mathcal{M}$.

Proof. Consider some system $\mathcal{M}$ and assume for the sake of a contradiction that there is a k-set agreement algorithm A for $\mathcal{M}$, sets of runs $\mathcal{R}_{(\bar{D})}$ and $\mathcal{R}_{(D,\bar{D})}$ and some sets of processes $D_1, \ldots, D_{k-1}$ such that (A)-(C) hold. These conditions imply that all processes in $\bar{D}$ decide in every run in $\mathcal{R}_{(D,\bar{D})}$, independently of the decision values of the processes in D. Observe that (dec-D) ensures that there are $\geq k-1$ distinct decision values in every run in $\mathcal{R}_{(D,\bar{D})}$. Due to (C) this implies the following fact:

(Fact 1) To guarantee k-agreement, all processes in $\bar{D}$ must decide on the same value, in all runs in $\mathcal{R}_{(\bar{D})}$. We will now show that this fact yields a contradiction.

Starting from $\mathcal{M}'_{A|\bar{D}}$ we know by (E) that for each $\rho' \in \mathcal{M}'_{A|\bar{D}}$, there exists a run $\rho \in \mathcal{M}_A$ such that $\rho' \stackrel{\bar{D}}{\sim} \rho$. Obviously no process $p \in \bar{D}$ receives messages from a process $q \in D$ in ρ' before p's decision (as such a process q does not exist in $\mathcal{M}'$); clearly this also holds for the indistinguishable run ρ. Therefore, we have that, in fact, $\rho \in \mathcal{R}_{(\bar{D})}$, and due to (Fact 1), we know that all processes decide on the same value in all runs $\rho' \in \mathcal{M}'_{A|\bar{D}}$. This, however, means that we could employ $A_{|\bar{D}}$ to solve consensus in $\mathcal{M}'$, which contradicts (D). □

There are several noteworthy points about Theorem 8.2.1:

- Our impossibility argument uses a 2-partitioning argument but does *not* require the system to (temporarily or permanently) decompose into $k+1$ partitions. In particular, there is no further restriction on the communication among processes within D, respectively within $\bar{D}$.

- The proof neither restricts the types of failures that can occur in $\mathcal{M}$ nor the underlying synchrony assumptions of $\mathcal{M}$ in any way.

- At a first glance, requirement (C) might appear to be redundant. After all, it should always be possible to find a run in $\mathcal{R}_{(D,\bar{D})}$ that is indistinguishable for the processes in $\bar{D}$, given some run in $\mathcal{R}_{(\bar{D})}$. We will now try to give an intution for its necessity; in the proof of Theorem 8.3.6 we will see that (C) is non-trivial in realistic settings.

  To see why (C) is necessary, first consider some run γ (of some algorithm in some model $\mathcal{M}$) that satisfies property (dec-D). This stipulates $k-1$ distinct decision values among the processes in D, which essentially means that γ was a quite "asynchronous" run for the processes in D. It could therefore be the case that the synchrony assumptions of $\mathcal{M}$ require γ to be "synchronous" for the processes in $\bar{D}$.

  Now suppose that we are a given a run $\alpha \in \mathcal{R}_{(\bar{D})}$ and we need to find a run $\beta \in \mathcal{R}_{(D,\bar{D})}$ that is indistinguishable for processes in $\bar{D}$, in order to make (C) hold. If α is an "asynchronous" run for the processes in $\bar{D}$, we might not be able to find a matching run $\beta \in \mathcal{R}_{(D,\bar{D})}$, as the above setting requires such runs to be "synchronous" for the processes in $\bar{D}$.

8.3. Applying Theorem 8.2.1

In this section we will apply Theorem 8.2.1 to various system models. More specifically, we will first apply our theorem to asynchronous message passing systems and then show that failure detector (Σ_k, Ω_k) (see Bonnet and Raynal, 2009, 2010b) is not sufficient for k-set agreement.

8.3.1. The Partially Synchronous Case

It is easy to show that k-set agreement is impossible in model $\mathcal{M}^{\text{ASYNC}}$ if we assume a wait-free environment, for any $k < n$, by simply partitioning the system into $|\Pi|$ partitions until every process has decided. No such simple method is known when things become more complicated: When, for example, f (i.e. the number of possible failures) is somewhat restricted and/or the model is partially synchronous, a more involved argument is necessary. We will now show how to avoid proving the impossibility "from scratch" by instantiating Theorem 8.2.1.[4]

Theorem 8.3.1
> There is no algorithm that solves k-set agreement in an asynchronous system $\mathcal{M}$ of n processes, for any
> $$k \leq \frac{n-1}{\ell}, \tag{8.1}$$
> where, from the $f = n - \ell$ possibly faulty processes, $f - 1$ can fail by crashing initially and 1 process can crash during the execution. This holds even if processes are synchronous in $\mathcal{M}$, communication is broadcast-based, and computing steps are atomic.

Proof (Theorem 8.3.1). Assume in contradiction that some f-resilient algorithm A solves k-set agreement. We will show that conditions (A)–(E) of Theorem 8.2.1 are satisfied, thus yielding a contradiction.

As a first step, we will identify suitable sets D_i such that (A)–(C) hold for the runs in $\mathcal{R}_{(\bar{D})}$, respectively $\mathcal{R}_{(D,\bar{D})}$. For $1 \leq i < k$, define $D_i = \{p_{(i-1)\ell+1}, \ldots, p_{i\ell}\}$ and let

$$D = \bigcup_{1 \leq i \leq k-1} D_i.$$

Note that the failure assumption (8.1) guarantees that these sets D_i exist.

Lemma 8.3.2. The set $\bar{D}$ contains at least $n - f + 1$ processes.

Proof. We are done if we can show that $|D| + n - f + 1 \leq n$, i.e.,

$$(k-1)(n-f) + (n-f+1) = k(n-f) + 1 = k\ell + 1 \leq n,$$

which matches exactly (8.1). $\square$

(A) Recalling that algorithm A is resilient to $f - 1$ initial crashes and tolerates up to 1 (normal) crash, it follows by Observation 8.1.2.(a) that A is $\{H \mid |H| \geq n - f\}$-independent and thus also $\{D_1, \ldots, D_{k-1}, \bar{D}\}$-independent. By virtue of Observation 8.1.2.(b), A is $\{\bar{D}\}$-independent, which implies (A).

(B) It suffices to realize that the set of runs, where all communication from processes in D to processes in $\bar{D}$ is delayed until every correct process in $\bar{D}$ has decided, is

---
[4]To ease the presentation of the theorem, we define $\ell = n - f$.

nonempty. Since communication is asynchronous, this set is obviously nonempty and thus $\mathcal{R}_{(\bar{D})}$ is nonempty.

(C) Consider the set of runs $\mathcal{H}$ where all communication between the sets of processes $D_1, \ldots, D_{k-1}, \bar{D}$ is delayed until every correct process has decided. Clearly $\mathcal{H} \subseteq \mathcal{R}_{(D,\bar{D})}$, and, for any $\rho \in \mathcal{R}_{(\bar{D})}$ we can easily find a matching run in $\mathcal{R}_{(D,\bar{D})}$ that is indistinguishable for all processes in $\bar{D}$, yielding (C).

(D) Now consider a system $\mathcal{M}' = \langle \bar{D} \rangle$ that has the same system assumptions as $\mathcal{M}$, with the restriction that at most 1 process can crash in $\mathcal{M}'$ at any time. Condition (D) follows immediately from the result of Dolev et al. (1987, Table I), since we have already shown in Lemma 8.3.2 that

$$|\bar{D}| \geqslant n - f + 1 \geqslant 2$$

and 1 process can crash in the runs of $\mathcal{M}'$.

(E) We will show that for every run $\rho' \in \mathcal{M}'_{A_{|\bar{D}}}$, there is a corresponding run $\rho \in \mathcal{M}_A$, such that $\rho' \overset{\bar{D}}{\sim} \rho$. Fix any $\rho' \in \mathcal{M}'_{A_{|\bar{D}}}$ and consider the run $\rho \in \mathcal{M}_A$ where every correct process in $\bar{D}$ has the same sequence of states in ρ as in ρ', and all remaining processes—of which there are $\leqslant f - 1$—are initially dead in ρ. Such a run ρ exists, since $A_{|\bar{D}}$ is the restriction of A (see Definition 8.0.1).

We can therefore apply Theorem 8.2.1 and conclude that A does not solve k-set agreement. (Proof of Theorem 8.3.1)□

8.3.2. Failure Detector (Σ_k, Ω_k)

While the asynchronous model is without doubt the classical setting for an impossibility result, it does not fully exploit the advantages of our approach. In this section we will demonstrate the full power of Theorem 8.2.1 by deriving a new result: We will show the impossibility of achieving k-set agreement with failure detector (Σ_k, Ω_k), which was thought to be a promising candidate for the corresponding weakest failure detector (see Bonnet and Raynal, 2009).[5]

We have already introduced failure detector Σ_k in Section 7.6 (see Definition 7.6.1). We will now restate the failure detector class Ω_k, which was introduced by Neiger (1995).[6]

---
[5]Despite the negative results of this section, Σ_k remains interesting in its own right, as it was shown by Bonnet and Raynal (2009) to be necessary for solving k-set agreement with any failure detector.
[6]Recall from Definition 2.2.1 (Page 24) that F denotes the set of faulty processes in a run.

Definition 8.3.3. The output of the *generalized leader oracle* Ω_k, for $1 \leq k \leq n-1$, satisfies the following properties:

- (Validity) For all processes p and all times t, history $H(p,t)$ is a set of k process identifiers.

- (Eventual Leadership) There exists a time t_{GST} and a set LD, such that

$$(LD \cap (\Pi \setminus F) \neq \emptyset) \wedge (\forall t \geq t_{\text{GST}} \; \forall p \colon H(p,t) = LD).$$

For our impossibility proof, we will make use of certain failure detector histories that allow up to k partitions.

Definition 8.3.4. Let $\{D_1, \ldots, D_{k-1}, \bar{D}\}$ be a partitioning of the processes in Π where $|\bar{D}| \geq k$, and let $D_k = \bar{D}$. We call a failure detector history H of $\langle \Sigma_k, \Omega_k \rangle$ a $\{D_1, \ldots, D_{k-1}, \bar{D}\}$-*partitioning history*, if the output of $\langle \Sigma_k, \Omega_k \rangle$ satisfies the following properties:

1. For $1 \leq i \leq k$, the output of Σ_k at every process in D_i is a valid history for $\Sigma \; (= \Sigma_1)$ in the restricted model $\mathcal{M}_i = \langle D_i \rangle$.

2. There exists some fixed point in time t_{GST} such that the following holds: Let LD_i^t denote the leader set that is output by Ω_k at process p_i, for some point in time t. For all $t < t_{\text{GST}}$ and for $p_j \in D_i$ we have that

$$LD_j^t \cap D_i \neq \emptyset, \tag{8.2}$$

if $1 \leq i \leq k-1$, whereas

$$LD_\ell^t \subseteq \bar{D},$$

for $p_\ell \in \bar{D}$. For all $t \geq t_{\text{GST}}$, the output of Ω_k is the same set LD at every process p and depends on the failure pattern F in a run:

   (a) If $\bar{D} \not\subseteq F$, then $LD_p^t \subseteq \bar{D}$.

   (b) If $\bar{D} \subseteq F$, then $LD_p^t \cap D_i \neq \emptyset$ and $LD_p^t \cap (\Pi \setminus F) \neq \emptyset$, for $1 \leq i \leq k$.

Lemma 8.3.5. *Every $\{D_1, \ldots, D_{k-1}, \bar{D}\}$-partitioning history of $\langle \Sigma_k, \Omega_k \rangle$ is a valid history for $\langle \Sigma_k, \Omega_k \rangle$.*

Proof. Consider an arbitrary finite stabilization time t_{GST}. Obviously the history satisfies the (Eventual Leadership) property of Ω_k, since the output stabilizes with respect to the failure pattern of a given run. The (validity) property of Ω_k holds by construction.

For Σ_k, choose any set P of $k+1$ of processes in Π. First, observe that the combined liveness conditions of the local Σ histories immediately imply that liveness holds for Σ_k (see Definition 7.6.1). By the pigeon principle, at least two processes of P must be in in the same set D_i, for some $1 \leqslant i \leqslant k$, where $D_k = \bar{D}$. Observing that the intersection property of Σ also implies that the history is valid for Σ_k completes the proof. □

Theorem 8.3.6

> There is no $(n-1)$-resilient algorithm that solves k-set agreement in an asynchronous system with failure detector $\langle \Sigma_k, \Omega_k \rangle$, for any
>
> $$3 \leqslant k \leqslant \left\lfloor \frac{n+1}{2} \right\rfloor. \tag{8.3}$$

Proof (Theorem 8.3.6). We assume by contradiction that there is such an algorithm A. We use the following partitioning of Π: Let $\bar{D} = \{p_1, \ldots, p_k\}$ and choose $D_1, \ldots, D_{k-1}$ such that they partition the set $\Pi \setminus \bar{D}$. Since (8.3) holds and

$$|\bar{D}| = k,$$

we have that

$$|D_1 \cup \cdots \cup D_{k-1}| \geqslant k - 1;$$

thus such a partitioning exists.

We will show the impossibility for the failure detector $\langle \Sigma'_k, \Omega'_k \rangle$, which restricts $\langle \Sigma_k, \Omega_k \rangle$ by allowing only $\{D_1, \ldots, D_{k-1}, \bar{D}\}$-partitioning histories.[7] Due to Lemma 8.3.5, $\langle \Sigma_k, \Omega_k \rangle$ is weaker than $\langle \Sigma'_k, \Omega'_k \rangle$; therefore, this impossibility carries over to $\langle \Sigma_k, \Omega_k \rangle$.

Lemma 8.3.7. Suppose that processes can query $\langle \Sigma'_k, \Omega'_k \rangle$. Then, algorithm A is $\{D_1, \ldots, D_{k-1}, \bar{D}\}$-independent.

Proof. Consider any D_i, for $1 \leqslant i \leqslant k$, where $D_k = D$ and assume in contradiction that there is a run α with history H_α and failure pattern F_α such that some correct process $p_i \in D_i$ does not decide. Also assume that p_i does not receive any messages

---
[7] Note that processes do not know this partitioning.

from processes in $\Pi \setminus D_i$ in α. Consider a run β with history H_β and failure pattern F_β where all processes not in D_i are initially dead. Let t_{p_i} be the time in β when the correct process p_i decides. Furthermore, every process $p_j \in D_i$ takes the same steps in α and β, and

$$H_\beta(p_j, t) = H_\alpha(p_j, t),$$
$$F_\beta = F_\alpha,$$
$$\forall t \colon F_\alpha(t) \cap D_i = F_\beta(t) \cap D_i,$$

for all $t \leqslant t_{p_i}$. The last condition guarantees that p_i will receive the same messages in both runs from the other processes in D_i. Such a run β exists, due to the facts that A is $n-1$ resilient and that the above restriction of H_β is a legitimate output of $\langle \Sigma'_k, \Omega'_k \rangle$. Since α and β are indistinguishable for process p_i, it must decide in α at time t_{p_i}, yielding a contradiction. □

(A) Together with Observation 8.1.2.(b), Lemma 8.3.7 immediately implies that A is $\{\bar{D}\}$-independent.

(B) Since there are runs in $\mathcal{M}_A$ where all processes except the ones in $\bar{D}$ are initially dead, the correctness of A implies that there are runs where processes in $\bar{D}$ decide without receiving any messages from processes in $D = \bigcup_{1 \leqslant i \leqslant k-1} D_i$. Thus $\mathcal{R}_{(\bar{D})} \neq \emptyset$, i.e. requirement (B) of Theorem 8.2.1 holds.

(C) Consider any run $\alpha \in \mathcal{R}_{(\bar{D})}$ with a (partitioning) failure detector history H_α and failure pattern F_α, and let $\mathcal{R} \subseteq \mathcal{R}_{(D,\bar{D})}$ be the set of runs where all communication between the sets of processes $D_1, \ldots, D_{k-1}, \bar{D}$ is delayed until every correct process has decided. Note that Lemma 8.3.7 guarantees that $\mathcal{R}$ is nonempty. By definition, α is such that a process $p \in \bar{D}$ does not receive messages from processes in D until after p has decided (or crashed). Let t_{dec} denote the time where every process in $\bar{D}$ has decided or crashed in α. We consider a run $\beta \in \mathcal{R}$ with the partitioning history H_β and failure pattern F_β, where processes in $\bar{D}$ take the same steps as in α until time t_{dec}, and

$$F_\alpha(t) \cap \bar{D} = F_\beta(t) \cap \bar{D},$$

for all times $t \leqslant t_{\text{dec}}$. Moreover, for all $p \in \bar{D}$, we assume that

$$H_\alpha(p, t) = H_\beta(p, t), \tag{8.4}$$

for all $t \leqslant t_{\text{dec}}$. Note carefully that we do not restrict H_β at processes in D in any way. Since H_α is a partitioning history, (8.4) reveals that H_β is a valid partitioning history for F_β as well. Furthermore, α and β are clearly indistinguishable for processes in $\bar{D}$ until time t_{dec}; recalling that $\beta \in \mathcal{R} \subseteq \mathcal{R}_{(D,\bar{D})}$ shows that $\alpha \stackrel{\bar{D}}{\sim} \beta$, and thus $\mathcal{R}_{(\bar{D})} \preceq_{\bar{D}} \mathcal{R}_{(D,\bar{D})}$.

(D) We will first choose an appropriately restricted model $\mathcal{M}'$; recall that

$$|\bar{D}| = k \geqslant 3.$$

That is, $\mathcal{M}' = \langle \bar{D} \rangle$ is an asynchronous system augmented with $\langle \Sigma'_k, \Omega'_k \rangle$ of size $\geqslant 3$ where $|\bar{D}| - 1$ processes fail by crashing. Since we are only considering partitioning histories, processes in $\mathcal{M}'$ effectively access a failure detector $\langle \Sigma, \Gamma \rangle$, where Γ satisfies the part of Definition 8.3.4 that concerns Ω_k, for the processes in $\bar{D}$: More specifically, Γ outputs a set of k process ids, which according to Definition 8.3.4 2.(a) is the whole set $\bar{D}$, since $\bar{D}$ contains at least one correct process. Obviously, Γ is implementable in a purely asynchronous system of size k, which means that the combination $\langle \Sigma, \Gamma \rangle$ is too weak for solving consensus.

(E) Finally, we note that for any run in $\mathcal{M}'_{A_{|\bar{D}}}$ there is a run in $\mathcal{R}_{(\bar{D})}$ where all processes in D are initially dead, and the processes in $\bar{D}$ take identical steps, fail at the same time, and receive the same failure detector output, i.e., $\mathcal{M}'_{A_{|\bar{D}}} \preceq_{\bar{D}} \mathcal{R}_{(\bar{D})}$ and hence $\mathcal{M}'_{A_{|\bar{D}}} \preceq_{\bar{D}} \mathcal{M}_A$.

Applying Theorem 8.2.1 yields the required contradiction. (Proof of Theorem 8.3.6)□

It is worth noting that Definition 8.3.4 (in particular 2.(a)) in conjunction with our freedom to choose a suitable failure environment for $\mathcal{M}'$ allows us to use the failure detector output for processes in $\bar{D}$ "as is", i.e., without modification, when making the transition from $\mathcal{M} = \langle \Pi \rangle$ to $\mathcal{M}' = \langle \bar{D} \rangle$.

Note that we explicitly need $k > 2$ in Theorem 8.3.6, since for $k = 2$ we have a system of two processes where Σ is equivalent to Ω and thus sufficient to solve consensus, as was shown by Delporte-Gallet et al. (2010).

8.4. Discussion

In this chapter we have introduced a generic way of characterizing the impossibility of k-set agreement in message passing systems. The main advantage of our approach is that we are independent of a specific system model, since Theorem 8.2.1 neither makes assumptions on the available amount of synchrony, nor on the power of computing steps, nor on the communication primitives available to processes.

Future work on this topic will involve

- identifying other settings where Theorem 8.2.1 can be applied,

- developing a general theory of T-independence for failure detectors and other message passing systems, and

- finding weak system models that provide just enough synchrony to circumvent impossibility.

Chapter 9

A Weak Communication Predicate for k-Set Agreement

> Honest disagreement is often a good sign of progress.
>
> *(Mahatma Gandhi)*

WE HAVE ALREADY SEEN two system models where $(n-1)$-set agreement is achievable by implementing failure detector $\mathcal{L}$, and have shown how to solve k-set agreement with $\mathcal{L}(k)$. In this chapter we will focus on solving the k-set agreement problem (see Section 7.1) in a round-based setting, where $1 \leqslant k < n$.[1] In the round model that we will introduce below, all processes are considered to be "internally" correct, although they may be perceived as faulty by other processes. We therefore actually consider the variant of k-set agreement where *all* processes must eventually decide. In this setting, "crashed" processes are modeled as processes from which no one else receives messages.

9.1. The Round Model

We assume that the computation is organized in an infinite sequence of communication-closed (Elrad and Francez, 1982) rounds; that is, any message sent in a round can be received only in that round. Using rounds instead of a synchrony assumption allows us to

---

[1]The results of this chapter are joint work with Martin Biely (see Biely et al., 2010a).

focus on what processes perceive instead of treating failures and asynchrony separately. This idea was introduced in a seminal paper by Santoro and Widmayer (1989) who coined the term "transmission fault", and is also prominent in the round models of Gafni (1998) and Charron-Bost and Schiper (2009), which were discussed in Section 1.3. Another example of a round-based model is the perception-based hybrid failure model (Schmid and Weiss, 2002; Biely et al., 2010b) where processes can experience a (bounded) amount of receive failures and send failures per round. Widder and Schmid (2007) extended this failure model to a variant of the Θ-Model (see Section 5.1) where processes do not startup simultaneously.

The round model that we have described so far shows little resemblance to the basic system assumptions introduced in Chapter 2, since untimely messages cannot be received in any later round and thus are lost. Nevertheless, we can outline a mapping for asynchronous runs to this round structure by making the following assumptions:

- Processes perform time-driven computations in a synchronous manner.

- Processes have read-access to some variable r that contains the current round number.

In order to be able to actually execute algorithms designed for the round model in such a system we need an additional layer of simulation:

- A messages that is sent is tagged with the value of r.

- The first time that p reads a new value of r, process p executes the round algorithm by providing all previously received messages tagged with $r-1$ as the input parameters of the transition function.

- Process p discards all messages that have a tagged value smaller than the current value of its round variable r (and buffers all messages with a tag value that is greater or equal).

This way asynchrony is transformed to message loss in the round.

As in the models of Gafni (1998) and Charron-Bost and Schiper (2009), we will express assumptions about the synchrony and the reliability of communication in a system by a predicate that characterizes the set of edges in the communication graph of each round. Intuitively speaking, there is an edge from process p to q in the communication graph of round r if q received p's round r message. We will in fact identify a system by its predicate, that is, in a system P the collections of communication graphs of each run

Chapter 9. A Communication Predicate for k-Set Agreement

of an algorithm in that system must fulfill predicate P. For example, a predicate that requires the communication graph of each round to be fully connected, corresponds to the synchronous (fault-free) model. Obviously, our goal is to find a weak predicate for k-set agreement that avoids such unnecessarily strong assumptions, i.e., a weak system model.

We now formally define computations in our round model. Algorithms are composed of two functions: The sending function determines, for each process p and round $r \geqslant 1$, the message p broadcasts in round r based on the p's state at the beginning of round r. Recall that we consider communication-closed rounds, which means that a message sent in round r cannot be received in any later round. The transition function determines, for each p and round r and the vector of messages received in r, the state at the end of round r, i.e., at the beginning of round $r + 1$. Clearly, a *run* of an algorithm is completely determined by the initial states of the processes and the sequence of communication graphs.

Definition 9.1.1. Consider round $r > 0$. We denote the *communication graph of round* r by $\mathcal{G}^r = \langle V, E^r \rangle$, where each node of the set V is associated with one process from Π, and where E^r is the set of directed *timely edges* for round r. There is an edge from p to q, denoted as $(p \to q)$, if and only if q receives p's round r message (in round r).

To simplify the presentation, we will denote a process and the associated node in the communication graph by the same symbols. We will write $p \in \mathcal{G}^r$ and $(p \to q) \in \mathcal{G}^r$ instead of $p \in V$ resp. $(p \to q) \in E^r$.

Definition 9.1.2. We denote the *stable skeleton graph of round* r by $\mathcal{G}^{\cap r}$ and define $\mathcal{G}^{\cap r} := \langle V, E^{\cap r} \rangle$ where

$$E^{\cap r} := \bigcap_{0 < r' \leqslant r} E^{r'}.$$

Intuitively speaking, $\mathcal{G}^{\cap r}$ is the subgraph consisting of the edges that have been timely in all rounds up to round r. The crucial property of $E^{\cap r}$ is that once an edge is untimely in some round r, it cannot be in $\mathcal{G}^{\cap r'}$, for any $r' \geqslant r$. That is,

$$\forall r > 0: E^{\cap r} \supseteq E^{\cap r+1},$$

which implies the subgraph relation

$$\forall r > 0: \mathcal{G}^{\cap r} \supseteq \mathcal{G}^{\cap r+1}. \tag{9.1}$$

Stable Skeleton Graphs and Timely Neighborhoods

We are particularly interested in certain graphs that model the perpetual timeliness throughout a run.

Definition 9.1.3. The *stable skeleton of a run*, is defined as the intersection[a] over all rounds, i.e.,

$$\mathcal{G}^{\cap\infty} := \bigcap_{r>0} \mathcal{G}^{\cap r}. \tag{9.2}$$

---
[a] For simplicity, we set $G \cap G' := \langle V \cap V', E \cap E' \rangle$.

Figures 9.1 and 9.2 show the stable skeleton of round 2 and of an entire run, respectively.

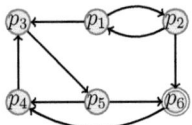

Figure 9.1.: $\mathcal{G}^{\cap 2}$

Considering that a run α consists of infinitely many rounds, whereas our system consists of only a finite number of processes, it follows that the number of possible distinct stable skeletons must also be finite. Consequently, the subgraph property (9.1) implies that there is some round r_{ST} when $\mathcal{G}^{\cap\infty}$ has *stabilized*, i.e.,

$$\forall r \geqslant r_{\text{ST}}: \mathcal{G}^{\cap r} = \mathcal{G}^{\cap\infty}.$$

The k-set agreement algorithm in Section 9.3 will approximate the stable skeleton of a run. The first step in this effort is to use the locally available information about the communication graph, which is captured by the notion of timely neighbourhoods.

Definition 9.1.4. The *timely neighborhood of p until round r*, denoted as $PT(p,r)$, is the set of processes that process p has perceived as *perpetually timely* until round r. Formally,

$$PT(p,r) := \{q \mid (q \to p) \in \mathcal{G}^{\cap r}\}.$$

In other words, p has received a message from every process in $PT(p,r)$ in every round up to and including r. Analogously to (9.1) and (9.2), we have

$$PT(p,r) \supseteq PT(p,r+1) \tag{9.3}$$

Chapter 9. A Communication Predicate for k-Set Agreement

and define

$$PT(p) := \bigcap_{r>0} PT(p, r). \tag{9.4}$$

We will make heavy use of the standard graph-theoretic notion of a *strongly connected component* of $\mathcal{G}^{\cap r}$. Note that we implicitly assume that strongly connected components are always nonempty and maximal. We use the superscript notation $\mathcal{C}^r$ when talking about a *strongly connected component of* $\mathcal{G}^{\cap r}$. Moreover, we write $\mathcal{C}_p^r$ to denote the (unique) strongly connected component of $\mathcal{G}^{\cap r}$ that contains process p in round r. The strongly connected component $\mathcal{C}_p^\infty \subseteq \mathcal{G}^{\cap \infty}$ that contains p in a run is defined analogously to (9.2) as

$$\mathcal{C}_p^\infty := \bigcap_{r>0} \mathcal{C}_p^r.$$

Note that when p and q are strongly connected in $\mathcal{G}^{\cap r}$, then they are also strongly connected in all $\mathcal{G}^{\cap r'}$, for $0 < r' \leqslant r$. From property (9.1) of $\mathcal{G}^{\cap r}$, we immediately have

$$\forall r > 0: \mathcal{C}_p^r \supseteq \mathcal{C}_p^{r+1}. \tag{9.5}$$

We will also use *directed paths* in $\mathcal{G}^{\cap r}$, where we assume that all nodes on a path are distinct.

Definition 9.1.5. Let $\mathcal{C}^r \subseteq \mathcal{G}^{\cap r}$ be a strongly connected component. $\mathcal{C}^r$ is a *root component in round r*, if

$$\forall p \in \mathcal{C}^r \; \forall q \in \mathcal{G}^{\cap r} : (q \to p) \in \mathcal{G}^{\cap r} \Rightarrow q \in \mathcal{C}^r.$$

Informally speaking, $\mathcal{C}^r$ is a root component if it has no incoming edges from any $q \in \mathcal{G}^{\cap r} \setminus \mathcal{C}^r$. Figure 9.2 shows a graph with 2 root components.

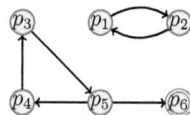

Figure 9.2.: The stable skeleton graph $\mathcal{G}^{\cap \infty}$ of an entire run. Each of the sets of processes $\{p_1, p_2\}$ and $\{p_3, p_4, p_5\}$ forms a root component in $\mathcal{G}^{\cap \infty}$.

Regarding the relation to the existing round-by-round models, we shortly recall what their predicates are based on: In the Heard-Of model (Charron-Bost and Schiper, 2009), for each round r and each process p, the set $HO(p,r)$ contains those processes that p hears from, i.e., receives a message from, in round r. In the case of the Round-by-Round Fault Detectors (Gafni, 1998), the output of p's fault detector in round r is referred to by $D(p,r)$. In each round r, process p waits until it receives a message from every process that is not contained in $D(p,r)$. While it is possible that p also receives a round r message from a process in $D(p,r)$, we assume that these messages are discarded. From this it is evident that we have the following correspondence between our skeleton graphs and the HO/RbR model:

$$(p \to q) \in E^{\cap r} \iff \begin{cases} \forall r' \leqslant r : p \in HO(q,r') \\ \forall r' \leqslant r : p \notin D(q,r') \end{cases} \tag{9.6}$$

Thus a process can determine its timely neighbourhood in the two models as follows:

$$PT(p,r) = \begin{cases} \bigcap_{0 < r' \leqslant r} HO(p,r') \\ \Pi \setminus \left(\bigcup_{0 < r' \leqslant r} D(p,r') \right) \end{cases} \tag{9.7}$$

As in the HO-model, we model a crashed processes by an "internally correct" process that no other process receives messages from after it has crashed (Charron-Bost and Schiper, 2009, Sec. 2.2). This modelling is the reason why we require all processes to decide. For a more detailed discussion on the relation between models where crashed processes actually stop and the HO-model, we refer to Hutle and Schiper (2007).

9.2. Predicate $\mathcal{P}_{\mathsf{srcs}}(k)$

In this section, we introduce a predicate that, together with Algorithm 6 in Section 9.3, is sufficient for solving k-set agreement.

For a run α, predicate $\mathcal{P}_{\mathsf{srcs}}(k)$ requires that in every set S of $k+1$ processes, there are two processes q, q' that receive timely messages from the same common process p, in every round. We say that p is a *2-source* and q, q' are *timely receivers of p* in α.

$$\mathcal{P}_{\mathrm{src}}(p,S) :: \exists q, q' \in S, q \neq q' : p \in (PT(q) \cap PT(q'))$$
$$\mathcal{P}_{\mathrm{srcs}}(k) :: \forall S, |S| = k+1 \ \exists p \in \Pi : \mathcal{P}_{\mathrm{src}}(p,S) \tag{9.8}$$

Note that p is not required to be distinct from q and q': $\mathcal{P}_{\mathsf{srcs}}(k)$ still holds if $p = q$, i.e., p always perceives itself in a timely fashion. Regarding communication graphs, this predicate ensures that any induced subgraph S of $\mathcal{G}^{\cap\infty}$ with $k+1$ nodes contains distinct nodes q and q', such that, for some node p, edges $(p \to q)$ and $(p \to q')$ exist (one of which may be a self-loop). Figure 9.2 shows the stable skeleton graph in a run where $\mathcal{P}_{\text{srcs}}(k)$ holds for $k = 3$.

At a first glance, it might appear that the perpetual nature of $\mathcal{P}_{\text{srcs}}(k)$ is an unnecessarily strong restriction. To see why some (possibly weak) perpetual synchrony is necessary, consider the predicate $\Diamond\mathcal{P}_{\text{srcs}}(k)$ that satisfies (9.8) just eventually, and suppose that there is an algorithm A that solves k-set agreement in system $\Diamond\mathcal{P}_{\text{srcs}}(k)$. Due to its "eventual" nature, $\Diamond\mathcal{P}_{\text{srcs}}(k)$ allows runs where *every* process forms a root component by itself, i.e., it receives no timely messages from other process, for a finite number of rounds. Moreover, for any k, the (infinite) run, where a *single* process forms a root component forever and thus has to decide on its own input value, is admissible. Using a simple indistinguishability argument, it is easy to show that processes decide on n different values.

The following result will be instrumental in Section 9.3, where we show how to solve k-set agreement with $\mathcal{P}_{\text{srcs}}(k)$. Note that Theorem 9.2.1 is independent of the algorithm employed.

Theorem 9.2.1

There are at most k root components in any run that is admissible in system $\mathcal{P}_{\text{srcs}}(k)$.

Proof. Assume by contradiction that there is a run α of some algorithm A that is admissible in system $\mathcal{P}_{\text{srcs}}(k)$, where there is a set of $\ell \geqslant k+1$ disjoint root components

$$R = \{\mathcal{C}_{p_1}^\infty, \ldots, \mathcal{C}_{p_\ell}^\infty\}$$

containing processes $p_1, \ldots, p_{k+1}, \ldots, p_\ell$. Let r be the round where every strongly connected root component $\mathcal{C}_{p_i}^\infty \in R$ has stabilized, i.e.,

$$\forall i \colon \mathcal{C}_{p_i}^r = \mathcal{C}_{p_i}^\infty.$$

That is, any two distinct root components in R must already be disjoint from round r on. Since α satisfies $\mathcal{P}_{\text{srcs}}(k)$ and $\ell \geqslant k+1$, there must be a 2-source p such that, for two distinct processes

$$p_i, p_j \in \{p_1, \ldots, p_{k+1}\},$$

it holds that

$$p \in (PT(p_i) \cap PT(p_j)).$$

By (9.6), it follows that the edges $e_i = (p \to p_i)$ and $e_j = (p \to p_j)$ are in $\mathcal{G}^{\cap r}$. Considering that $C_{p_i}^r$ and $C_{p_j}^r$ are root components by assumption, i.e., do not have incoming edges, it must be that $e_i \in C_{p_i}^r$ and $e_j \in C_{p_j}^r$, and therefore

$$p \in C_{p_i}^r \cap C_{p_j}^r.$$

This, however, contradicts the fact that $C_{p_i}^r$ and $C_{p_j}^r$ are disjoint, which completes our proof. □

Impossibility of $(k-1)$-Set Agreement

We will now show that $\mathcal{P}_{\mathrm{srcs}}(k)$ does *not* allow to solve $(k-1)$-set agreement. More specifically, we will prove this by assuming the existence of such an algorithm A, and then construct a run fulfilling $\mathcal{P}_{\mathrm{srcs}}(k)$ where processes decide on k (instead of $k-1$) different values.

Theorem 9.2.2

> Consider any k such that $1 < k < n$. There is no algorithm A that solves $(k-1)$-set agreement in system $\mathcal{P}_{\mathrm{srcs}}(k)$.

Proof. Assume for the sake of a contradiction that such an algorithm A exists. Suppose that all processes start with pairwise distinct input values. Consider the run α and a fixed set L of $k-1$ processes that only hear from themselves, formally speaking,

$$\forall p \in L \colon PT(p) = \{p\}.$$

Moreover, there is one process s such that every process not in L only hears from itself and s, i.e.,

$$\forall p \in \Pi \setminus L \colon PT(p) = \{p, s\}.$$

By *validity* and *termination* (see Section 9.3), processes eventually have to decide on some input value and processes in $L \cup \{s\}$ cannot learn any other process' input value, thus they have to decide on their own value. Thus, we have k different decision values, as we have assumed a unique input value for each process, and therefore a violation of $(k-1)$-*agreement*.

What remains to be shown is that this run α actually fulfills $\mathcal{P}_{\mathrm{srcs}}(k)$. Recall equation (9.8), i.e., the definition of $\mathcal{P}_{\mathrm{srcs}}$, and consider for any set S of size $k+1$ the set $P = S \setminus L$.

Since $|S \setminus L| \geq 2$, the set P contains at least two distinct processes that permanently receive timely messages from s (one of which may be s). That is, process s is the required 2-source for any set S of $k+1$ processes. □

9.3. Approximating the Stable Skeleton Graph and Solving k-Set Agreement

In this section, we present and analyze an algorithm that solves k-set agreement with predicate $\mathcal{P}_{\text{srcs}}(k)$. Algorithm 6 employs a generic approximation of the stable skeleton graph of the run, which works as follows: First, every process p keeps track of the processes it has perceived as timely until round r in the set PT_p, updated in Line 9. Lemma 9.3.2 will show that PT_p satisfies the definition of $PT(p,r)$, for all rounds r. In addition, every process p locally maintains an approximation graph G_p of the stable skeleton, denoted G_p^r for round r, which is broadcast in every round. If a process q receives such a graph G_p^r from some process p in its timely neighborhood $PT(q,r)$, it adds the information contained in G_p^r to its own local approximation G_q^r. Note that, in contrast to the stable skeleton graph $\mathcal{G}^{\cap r}$, the approximation graph G_p is actually a *weighted* directed graph. The edge labels of G_p correspond to the round number when a particular edge was added by some process, i.e., the edge $(q' \xrightarrow{r} q)$ is in G_p if, and only if, $q' \in PT(q,r)$ (cf. Lemma 9.3.2(b)). To prevent outdated information from remaining in the approximation graph permanently, every process p purges all edges in G_p^r that were initially added more than $n-1$ rounds ago. Figures 9.3a-9.3f show this approximation mechanism at work.

For k-set agreement, process p only considers proposal values for its estimated decision value x_p that were sent by processes in its current timely neighborhood, i.e., in PT_p. This ensures that p and q will have a common estimated decision value $x_p = x_q$ in round n, if they are in the same strongly connected component (cf. Lemma 9.3.14). To determine when to terminate, p analyzes its approximation graph in every round $r \geq n$ and decides if G_p^r is a strongly connected graph.

Why is this decision safe with respect to the agreement property? Using our graph approximation results, we will show in Lemma 9.3.15 that any strongly connected approximation graph contains at least one root component in the stable skeleton graph. Furthermore, if two processes decide on different values, it follows that their approximated graphs in the rounds of their respective decision are disjoint. Since Theorem 9.2.1

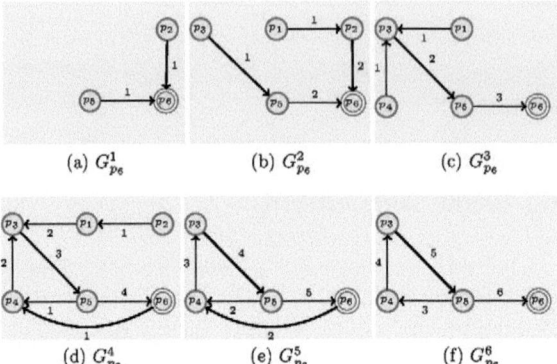

Figure 9.3.: Figures 9.3a-9.3f show the local approximation of $\mathcal{G}^{\cap \infty}$ depicted in Figure 9.2 (Page 127) and of $\mathcal{G}^{\cap 2}$ (Figure 9.1, Page 126) during rounds 1 to 6 by process p_6. For simplicity, we omit self-loops that is we assume that every process always perceives itself as timely, formally, $\forall p_i : p_i \in PT(p_i)$.

confirms that there are at most k root components in any run where $\mathcal{P}_{\text{srcs}}(k)$ holds, there can be in fact at most k different decision values.

9.3.1. Approximation of the Stable Skeleton Graph

Throughout our analysis, we denote the value of variable var of process p at the end of round r as var_p^r. When we use the subgraph relation ($\subseteq$) between graphs C_p^r and G_p^r, we mean the standard subgraph relation between C_p^r and the *unweighted* version of G_p^r. We first state some obvious facts that follow directly from the code of the algorithm:

Observation 9.3.1. *For any round $r > 0$ it holds that $p \in G_p^r$ and that no edge $(q' \xrightarrow{r'} q) \in G_p^r$ has $r' \leqslant r - n$.*

Note that, after the initial assignment, p only updates variable PT_p in Line 9, which is equivalent to (9.7). From this and the inspection of Lines 14 and 16, Lemma 9.3.2 follows immediately:

Lemma 9.3.2. *It holds that $q \in PT(p, r)$ if, and only if, all of the following are true:*

(a) $q \in PT_p^r$,

(b) *p adds a directed edge $q \xrightarrow{r} p$ to G_p^r by executing Line 16 in round r, and*

CHAPTER 9. A COMMUNICATION PREDICATE FOR k-SET AGREEMENT

Algorithm 6 Approximating the stable skeleton graph and solving k-set agreement with $\mathcal{P}_{\mathrm{srcs}}(k)$

Variables and Initialization:
1: $PT_p \in 2^\Pi$ initially Π
2: $x_p \in \mathbb{N}$ initially v_p // Estimated decision value
3: $G_p := \langle V_p, E_p \rangle$ initially $\langle \{p\}, \emptyset \rangle$ // weighted digraph
4: $decided_p \in \{0, 1\}$ initially 0 // is 1 iff p has decided

Round r: sending function S_p^r:
5: **if** $decided_p = 1$ **then**
6: $\quad$ send $(decide, x_p, G_p)$ to all processes
7: **else**
8: $\quad$ send $(prop, x_p, G_p)$ to all processes

Round r: transition function T_p^r:
9: update PT_p
10: **if** received $(decide, x_q, \_)$ from $q \in PT_p$ and $decided_p = 0$ **then**
11: $\quad x_p \leftarrow x_q$
12: $\quad$ decide on x_p
13: $\quad decided_p \leftarrow 1$

14: $G_p \leftarrow \langle \{p\}, \emptyset \rangle$
15: **for** $q \in PT_p$ **do**
16: $\quad$ add directed edge $(q \xrightarrow{r} p)$ to E_p
17: $\quad V_p \leftarrow V_p \cup V_q$
18: **for** every pair of nodes $(p_i, p_j) \in V_p \times V_p$ **do**
19: $\quad R_{i,j} \leftarrow \{r_e \mid \exists q \in PT_p : (p_i \xrightarrow{r_e} p_j) \in E_q\}$
20: $\quad$ **if** $R_{i,j} \neq \emptyset$ **then**
21: $\quad\quad r_{max} \leftarrow \max(R_{i,j})$
22: $\quad\quad E_p \leftarrow E_p \cup \{(p_i \xrightarrow{r_{max}} p_j)\}$
23: discard all $(p_i \xrightarrow{r_e} p_j)$ from E_p where $r_e \leqslant r - n$
24: discard $p_i \neq p$ from V_p if p is unreachable from p_i

25: **if** $decided_p = 0$ **then**
26: $\quad x_p \leftarrow \min\{x_q \mid q \in PT_p\}$
27: $\quad$ **if** $r \geqslant n$ and G_p is strongly connected **then**
28: $\quad\quad$ decide on x_p
29: $\quad\quad decided_p \leftarrow 1$

(c) for any $r' \neq r$, there is no other edge $q \xrightarrow{r'} p$ in G_p^r.

The following lemma shows that the approximation graph $G_{p_{\ell+1}}$ accurately reflects the timely neighborhood of a process. That is, if p_1 is connected to $p_{\ell+1}$ through a path of length ℓ, then $p_{\ell+1}$ will add the timely neighborhood information of p_1 to its approximated graph by round ℓ.

Lemma 9.3.3. *Suppose that there exists a directed path*

$$\Gamma = (p_1 \to \ldots \to p_{\ell+1})$$

in $\mathcal{G}^{\cap r}$ for round $r \geqslant n$, where Γ has length $\ell \leqslant n-1$. Then, for all $q \in PT(p_1, r-\ell)$ it holds that

(a) *edge* $(q \xrightarrow{r_q} p_1)$ *is in* $G^r_{p_{\ell+1}}$ *where* $r \geqslant r_q \geqslant r - \ell$, *and*

(b) $G^r_{p_{\ell+1}}$ *contains no other edges from q to p_1.*

Proof. Consider an arbitrary $q \in PT(p_1, r - \ell)$. The proof proceeds by induction over the edges of path Γ indexed by k. That is, we show that for all k, with $0 \leqslant k \leqslant \ell$, it holds that there is an edge $e = (q \xrightarrow{r_k} p_1)$ in $G^{r-\ell+k}_{p_{1+k}}$ where

$$r - \ell + k \geqslant r_k \geqslant r - \ell.$$

For the base case ($k = 0$), we have to show that the edge e is in $G^{r-\ell}_{p_1}$, but this already follows from $q \in PT(p_1, r - \ell)$, by Lemma 9.3.2.

For the induction step, we assume that the statement holds for some $k < \ell$ and then show that it holds for $k + 1$ as well. In round $r - \ell + (k+1)$ process p_{1+k} broadcasts its current graph estimate, i.e., $G^{r-\ell+k}_{p_{1+k}}$ to all. We know that $p_{1+(k+1)}$ will receive this message since $(p_{1+k} \to p_{1+(k+1)})$ is in the path $\Gamma \subseteq \mathcal{G}^{\cap r}$, which means that

$$p_{1+k} \in PT(p_{1+(k+1)}, r - \ell + (k+1)).$$

By the induction hypothesis, the edge $(q \xrightarrow{r_k} p_1)$ is in $G^{r-\ell+k}_{p_{1+k}}$ and therefore will be among the edges that $p_{1+(k+1)}$ considers in Line 19. This in turn implies that $p_{1+(k+1)}$ will add an edge $q \xrightarrow{r_{k+1}} p_1$ to its graph $G^{r-\ell+(k+1)}_{p_{1+(k+1)}}$ in Line 22, whereby r_{k+1} is calculated in Line 21 such that $r_{k+1} \geqslant r_k$. Moreover, by induction hypothesis we have

$$r_k \geqslant r - \ell > r - n,$$

which ensures that the edge will not be discarded in Line 23. Since the code following the for-loop in Line 18 is executed exactly once for every edge, no other edge $q \xrightarrow{r'} p_1$ is added to $G_{p_1+(k+1)}^{r-\ell+(k+1)}$. This completes the proof our lemma. □

The next lemma shows that the approximation graph of correctly (over)estimates the strongly connected component from round n on:

Lemma 9.3.4. *Let $r \geqslant n$ and consider the strongly connected component $\mathcal{C}_p^r$ containing p in $\mathcal{G}^{\cap r}$. Then, it holds that $G_p^r \supseteq \mathcal{C}_p^r$.*

Proof. Consider any edge $(q' \to q) \in \mathcal{C}_p^r$. Since $\mathcal{C}_p^r$ is strongly connected, there is a directed path between any pair of processes in $\mathcal{C}_p^r$, in particular there is a path of length $\ell \leqslant n-1$ from q to p. By the definition of $\mathcal{C}_p^r$ we know that q always perceives q' as timely in all rounds up to round r, which means that

$$q' \in PT(q, r - \ell).$$

Then, by applying Lemma 9.3.3, we get that the edge $(q' \xrightarrow{r'} q)$ is in G_p^r, for some

$$r' \geqslant r - \ell,$$

which shows that $\mathcal{C}_p^r$ is a subgraph of G_p^r. □

Lemma 9.3.2 showed that the timely neighborhood is eventually in the approximated graph. We now show that our approximation contains only valid information:

Lemma 9.3.5. *Let $r \geqslant 1$ and suppose that there is an edge $e = (q' \xrightarrow{r'} q)$ in the approximated stable skeleton graph G_p^r of process p. Then it holds that $q' \in PT(q, r')$.*

Proof. Note that processes only add edges to their approximation graphs in Line 16 or in Line 22. If an edge is added via Line 22, then this edge has previously been added by another process by executing Line 16. Therefore, every edge must have been added by some process via Line 16. For edge e, this process can only be q. By Lemma 9.3.2 this happens in round r' and $q' \in PT(q, r')$. □

The following Lemma 9.3.6 is in some sense the converse result of Lemma 9.3.4, as it states that the approximated graph must approach $\mathcal{C}_p^r$ from below, if it is strongly connected:

Lemma 9.3.6. *Let $r \geqslant 1$ and consider the strongly connected component $\mathcal{C}_p^r$. If the approximated skeleton graph G_p^{r+n-1} is strongly connected, then*

$$\mathcal{C}_p^r \supseteq G_p^{r+n-1}.$$

Proof. Consider any edge

$$e = (q' \xrightarrow{r'} q) \in G_p^{r+n-1}.$$

By Lemma 9.3.5, we know that $q' \in PT(q, r')$. It follows by the subset property (9.3) that $q' \in PT(q, r)$, as Observation 9.3.1 implies

$$r' > (r + n - 1) - n = r - 1.$$

Therefore, there is an edge $(q' \to q)$ in $\mathcal{G}^{\cap r}$. It follows that G_p^{r+n-1} is isomorphic to a (not necessarily maximal) strongly connected component $\mathcal{S}^r$ in $\mathcal{G}^{\cap r}$. Because $\mathcal{C}_p^r$ and $\mathcal{S}^r$ both contain p, their intersection is nonempty, i.e.,

$$\mathcal{C}_p^r \supseteq G_p^{r+n-1}.$$

□

As a final result about the approximated skeleton graph, we show that once the approximation G_p^r is strongly connected in round $r \geqslant n$, it is closed w.r.t. strongly connected components. This means that G_p^r can be partitioned into disjoint strongly connected components in $\mathcal{G}^{\cap \infty}$.

Theorem 9.3.7

Suppose that $R \geqslant n$. If the approximated skeleton graph G_p^R is strongly connected, then it contains the strongly connected component $\mathcal{C}_q^\infty$ of every $q \in G_p^R$.

Proof. Consider any $q \in G_p^R$ and its strongly connected component $\mathcal{C}_q^\infty$. From (9.5) and Lemma 9.3.6 it follows that

$$q \in G_p^R \subseteq \mathcal{C}_p^{R-n+1} \subseteq \mathcal{C}_p^1,$$

i.e., $q \in \mathcal{C}_p^1 \cap \mathcal{C}_q^1$.

Chapter 9. A Communication Predicate for k-Set Agreement

Now suppose the theorem does not hold. Then there exists some $q' \in \mathcal{C}_q^\infty$ such that $q' \notin G_p^R$. Due to Lemma 9.3.4, q' cannot be contained in $\mathcal{C}_p^R$, but due to (9.5),

$$q' \in \mathcal{C}_q^R \supseteq \mathcal{C}_q^\infty.$$

Therefore, $\mathcal{C}_q^R \neq \mathcal{C}_p^R$, and thus

$$\mathcal{C}_q^R \cap \mathcal{C}_p^R = \emptyset.$$

Since G_p^R is strongly connected and contains q, it also contains a path

$$\Gamma = (q = p_\ell \to \cdots \to p_0 = p),$$

such that

$$\forall i,\ 0 \leqslant i < \ell\colon p_{i+1} \in PT(p_i, R - i).$$

Let j be the minimal index i such that $p_j \in \mathcal{C}_q^R$, and let

$$\Gamma_j = (p_j \to \cdots \to p_0)$$

be the path remaining from p_j.

As both q' and p_j are in $\mathcal{C}_q^R$, there is a path Γ' in $\mathcal{C}_q^R$. Let k be the length of this path. Moreover, by applying Lemma 9.3.3, we get that $G_{p_j}^{R-j}$ contains the outgoing edge e of q' on this path, labeled with some round

$$r' \geqslant R - j - k. \tag{9.9}$$

But then, by the definition of Γ, it follows that when G_p^R contains p_j — which it does — then it must also contain q', unless some process p_i ($i < j$) removed e from its set of edges in Line 23 in round $R - i$ because

$$r' \leqslant R - i - n.$$

Since round R at process $p(= p_0)$ is the latest round when this can occur, we get that $r' \leqslant R - n$, and thus, by (9.9),

$$R - j - k \leqslant r' \leqslant R - n,\ \text{i.e.,}\ j + k \geqslant n. \tag{9.10}$$

Let Δ be the subgraph obtained by concatenating paths Γ' and Γ_j. By construction, Γ_j and Γ' only share node p_j, and thus Δ is a (simple) path and must have length

$$j + k \leqslant n - 1,$$

as no path can exceed length $n-1$. This contradicts (9.10) and thus completes the proof that q' is in G_p^R. The proof showing that all edges of $\mathcal{C}_q^\infty$ are in G_p^R proceeds analogously, by assuming that some edge in $\mathcal{C}_q^\infty$ ending in q' is not in G_p^R. □

9.3.2. k-Set Agreement

In this section, we will show that Algorithm 6 not only approximates the stable skeleton graph, but also solves k-set agreement. Our previous results allow us to immediately prove the validity and the termination properties.

Lemma 9.3.8 (Validity). *If a process decides on v, then v was the initial value of some process.*

Proof. Observe that the decision value x_p of any process p is initially set to its proposal value v_p, which is then broadcast. On all subsequent updates of x_p in Line 26, a value x_q that was sent by some process q (which originated from some $v_{q'}$) is assigned, therefore *validity* holds. □

Lemma 9.3.9. *Every process decides at most once in any run.*

Proof. Observe that no process executes Line 28 and Line 12 in the same run. This is guaranteed by the fact that process p cannot pass the if-conditions in Line 10 or in Line 25 after *decided$_p$* is set to 1, which happens whenever p decides. □

Lemma 9.3.10 (Termination). *Every process decides exactly once.*

Proof. Lemma 9.3.9 shows that every process decides at most once. We will now show that every process decides at least once. First, we will show that there is a root component in every round. Consider the strongly connected components that partition the set of nodes of the stable skeleton graph $\mathcal{G}^{\cap r}$ in some round r. Such a set always exists, since the strongly connected components form equivalence classes of nodes. It is well known that the contraction of the strongly connected components results in a directed acyclic graph, which reveals that there is at least one node $\mathcal{C}^r$ in the contracted graph that has no incoming edges. Clearly, $\mathcal{C}^r$ satisfies the definition of a root component

Chapter 9. A Communication Predicate for k-Set Agreement

in $\mathcal{G}^{\cap r}$. Therefore, there is a nonempty set R^r of strongly connected components all of which are root components in round r.

Let $r \geqslant 1$ be the earliest round where $\mathcal{G}^{\cap r}$ is stable for at least $n - 1$ rounds, i.e.,

$$\forall r' \in [r, r+n-1]: \mathcal{G}^{\cap r'} = \mathcal{G}^{\cap r}.$$

Note that property (9.1) implies that r exists. Now, consider any root component $\mathcal{R}^r \in R^r$: Clearly, since every process is in exactly one strongly connected component, we have

$$\forall p \in \mathcal{R}^r: \mathcal{C}_p^r = \mathcal{R}^r = \mathcal{R}^{r+n-1} = \mathcal{C}_p^{r+n-1}. \tag{9.11}$$

We will now show that the approximated skeleton graph of such a process p is in fact exactly the strongly connected component of p. Consider any $p \in \mathcal{R}^r (= \mathcal{C}_p^{r+n-1})$. First, since

$$r + n - 1 \geqslant n,$$

Lemma 9.3.4 and (9.11) imply that

$$\mathcal{R}^r \subseteq G_p^{r+n-1}.$$

We will now show that $\mathcal{R}^r \supseteq G_p^{r+n-1}$, which proves that these graphs are equal: Since G_p^{r+n-1} is connected by construction, it is sufficient to show that every edge in G_p^{r+n-1} is also in $\mathcal{R}^r$. Assume in contradiction that there is an edge

$$e = (q' \xrightarrow{r'} q) \in G_p^{r+n-1}$$

such that $q \in \mathcal{R}^r$ but $q' \notin \mathcal{R}^r$; note that the other way round ($q' \in \mathcal{R}^r$ but $q \notin \mathcal{R}^r$) is impossible by construction. Using Lemma 9.3.5 we know that $q' \in PT(q, r')$, and Observation 9.3.1 implies that

$$r' > (r + n - 1) - n = r - 1,$$

i.e., $r' \geqslant r$. Then, by definition, we have that $e \in \mathcal{G}^{\cap r}$, i.e., e is an incoming edge of $\mathcal{R}^r$, contradicting the assumption that $\mathcal{R}^r$ is a root component. We can therefore conclude that

$$\mathcal{R}^r = G_p^{r+n-1}.$$

By assumption, $\mathcal{R}^r$ is a root component, which tells us that G_p^{r+n-1} is strongly connected, i.e., p will pass the if-condition in Line 27 in round $r+n-1$ and decide. Recall the contracted stable skeleton graph of round $r+n-1$. Since every path in this graph is rooted at some node corresponding to a root component in the set R^r, it follows that all processes that are not in a root component will receive a decision message by round $r+2n-1$ and also decide, which completes our proof. □

In the remainder of this section we will prove that Algorithm 6 satisfies the *k-agreement* property. We will start out with some basic invariants on decision estimates.

Observation 9.3.11 (Monotonicity). *In any run of Algorithm 6 it holds that*
$$\forall r > 0\colon x_p^r \geqslant x_p^{r+1}.$$

Lemma 9.3.12. *If process p does not decide in Line 12, we have*
$$\forall r \geqslant n-1\colon x_p^r = x_p^{r+1}.$$

Proof. Suppose that there is an $r \geqslant n-1$ such that p sets $x_p^{r+1} \leftarrow x_q$ and $x_p^r \neq x_q$. This can only occur in Line 26, if the process does not decide in Line 12. From Observation 9.3.11 and *validity* (cf. Lemma 9.3.8), we know that p did not previously receive x_q and that x_q is the initial value of some distinct process q. Since processes forward their estimated decision value in every round, (9.3) implies that the shortest path from q to p (along which x_p has been propagated to p) in $\mathcal{G}^{\cap r+1}$ has length $r+1$. However, this is impossible as $r+1 \geqslant n$ and the longest possible path has length $n-1$. □

Lemma 9.3.13. *Suppose that some process p decides on x_p in round r by executing Line 12. Then some process $q \neq p$ has decided on x_p in round $r' < r$ by executing Line 28.*

Proof. Every process decides either in Line 28 or in Line 12, but not both (Lemma 9.3.9). Since p decided in Line 12 it must have received a $(decide, x_q, \_)$ message from some distinct process q. If q decided in Line 28 we are done; otherwise q decided in Line 12 in round $r-1$, we can repeat the same argument for q. After at most $n-1$ iterations, we arrive at some process that must have decided using Line 28. □

Lemma 9.3.14. *Let $\mathcal{C}_p^n$ be the strongly connected component of process p in round n. Then, it holds that*
$$\forall q \in \mathcal{C}_p^n\colon x_q^n = x_p^n.$$

Proof. First, observe that due to Lemma 9.3.13 and the fact that no process can pass the check in Line 27 before round n, no process can decide before round n. Therefore, processes can update their estimate values until at least round n.

Suppose that there are processes $p, q \in \mathcal{C}_p^n$, such that $x_p^n \neq x_q^n$. In particular we assume without loss of generality, that x_q^n is minimal among all round n estimation values of processes in $\mathcal{C}_p^r$, i.e., $x_p^n > x_q^n$.

Let r_q be the round where q first sets x_q to the value x_q^n. By Observation 9.3.11 it follows that q does not update x_q anymore before round n. Since Algorithm 6 satisfies *validity* (Lemma 9.3.8), we know that there is some process s that is the source of this value, i.e., s initially proposed x_q^r. By the code of the algorithm we know that in round r process p only considers values in Line 26 that were sent by some process in $PT(p,r)$. This implies that there is a sequence of pairwise distinct processes

$$s = q_1, \ldots, q_\ell = q,$$

such that

$$\forall i, (1 \leqslant i < \ell): q_i \in PT(q_{i+1}, i). \tag{9.12}$$

Clearly, $r_q = \ell - 1$. Let $j \leqslant \ell$ be such that $q_j \in \mathcal{C}_p^n$ and j is minimal, let Γ_q be the path in $\mathcal{G}^{\cap 1}$ induced by the sequence s up to q_j. Moreover, since $q_j \in \mathcal{C}_p^n$, there is a path Γ_p in $\mathcal{C}_p^n$ from q_j to p. Since

$$\mathcal{C}_p^n \subseteq \mathcal{G}^{\cap 1},$$

Γ_p is a path in $\mathcal{G}^{\cap 1}$ as well. Let Γ be the path in $\mathcal{G}^{\cap 1}$ obtained by appending Γ_p to Γ_q. By construction Γ is simple, and therefore its length is bounded by $n-1$. Moreover, the initial value of s was propagated along this path — over Γ_q by construction and over Γ_p, because x_q^n is minimal in $\mathcal{C}_p^n$. This leads to process p assigning this value to x_p in some round

$$r_p \leqslant n-1,$$

which contradicts the assumption that $x_p^n > x_q^n$. □

Lemma 9.3.15 (*k*-Agreement). *Processes decide on at most k distinct values.*

Proof (Lemma 9.3.15). For the sake of a contradiction, assume that there is a set of $\ell > k$ processes

$$D = \{p_1, \ldots, p_\ell\}$$

in a run α where p_i decides on $x_i^\infty = x_i^{r_i}$ [2] in round $r_i \geq n$ and

$$\forall p_i, p_j \in D \colon x_{p_i}^\infty \neq x_{p_j}^\infty.$$

By virtue of Lemma 9.3.13, we can assume that every p_i has decided by executing Line 28. Considering that no process decides before round n, applying Lemma 9.3.12 yields that

$$\forall r \geq n \ \forall p_i, p_j \in D \colon x_{p_i}^r \neq x_{p_j}^r. \tag{9.13}$$

Note that the approximated skeleton graphs $G_{p_i}^{r_i}$ and $G_{p_j}^{r_j}$ are strongly connected in round r_i resp. r_j, otherwise the processes could not have passed the if-condition before Line 28.

We will first show that the different decision values of p_i and p_j imply that their approximated skeleton graphs in rounds r_i resp. r_j are disjoint. Lemma 9.3.6 reveals that these skeleton graphs are contained within the respective strongly connected components of an earlier round, i.e.,

$$\mathcal{C}_{p_i}^{r_i-n+1} \supseteq G_{p_i}^{r_i} \text{ and } \mathcal{C}_{p_j}^{r_j-n+1} \supseteq G_{p_j}^{r_j}.$$

If these strongly connected components of p_i and p_j are disjoint, then so are the approximated skeleton graphs and we are done. Therefore, assume in contradiction that

$$I = \mathcal{C}_{p_i}^{r_i-n+1} \cap \mathcal{C}_{p_j}^{r_j-n+1} \neq \emptyset.$$

We will now prove that one of these components contains the other. Without loss of generality, suppose that $r_i \leq r_j$ and consider any node

$$p \in I \subseteq \mathcal{C}_{p_j}^{r_j-n+1}.$$

Clearly, p is strongly connected to every node in $\mathcal{C}_{p_j}^{r_j-n+1}$. Let $\mathcal{Z}$ be the induced subgraph of $\mathcal{C}_{p_j}^{r_j-n+1}$ in the skeleton graph $\mathcal{G}^{\cap r_i-n+1}$. By the subgraph property (9.5) and since $r_i \leq r_j$, it follows that

$$\mathcal{Z} = \mathcal{C}_{p_j}^{r_j-n+1},$$

and hence

$$\mathcal{Z} \cap \mathcal{C}_{p_i}^{r_i-n+1} \neq \emptyset.$$

---

[2] Note that x_p^∞ denotes p's final "estimate", i.e., the actual decision value of process p.

By the fact that $p \in I$, we know that $p \in \mathcal{C}_{p_i}^{r_i-n+1}$. That is, in the skeleton graph $\mathcal{G}^{\cap r_i-n+1}$, process p is strongly connected to all nodes in $\mathcal{C}_{p_i}^{r_i-n+1}$ and $\mathcal{Z}$. But since the strongly connected component $\mathcal{C}_{p_i}^{r_i-n+1}$ is maximal, we actually have

$$\mathcal{C}_{p_i}^{r_i-n+1} \supseteq \mathcal{Z} = \mathcal{C}_{p_j}^{r_j-n+1},$$

which means that $p_j \in \mathcal{C}_{p_i}^{r_i-n+1}$. Then, Lemma 9.3.14 readily implies that $\forall q \in \mathcal{C}_{p_i}^{r_i-n+1}$ it holds that $x_{p_i}^n = x_q^n$ and, in particular,

$$x_{p_i}^n = x_{p_j}^n,$$

which contradicts (9.13). We can therefore conclude that the intersection of the strongly connected components, and therefore, by Lemma 9.3.6, also the intersection of $G_p^{r_i}$ and $G_{p_j}^{r_j}$ is indeed empty, i.e.,

$$\forall p_i, p_j \in D \colon (G_{p_i}^{r_i} \cap G_{p_j}^{r_j}) = \emptyset. \tag{9.14}$$

By Theorem 9.3.7 it follows that each of the strongly connected approximated skeleton graphs $G_{p_i}^{r_i}$ can be partitioned into a set D_i of strongly connected components in $\mathcal{G}^{\cap \infty}$. Note that (9.14) implies that no strongly connected component is in two distinct sets D_i, D_j.

Lemma 9.3.16. Every set of strongly connected components D_i contains a root component, for $1 \leqslant i \leqslant \ell$.

Proof. For the sake of a contradiction, assume that (w.l.o.g.) the set D_ℓ corresponding to $G_{p_\ell}^{r_\ell}$ does not contain a root component. Now consider the contracted graph of $\mathcal{G}^{\cap \infty}$ where the nodes are the strongly connected components. Since the contracted graph is acyclic, it follows that there exists a path Γ in the (non-contracted) graph $\mathcal{G}^{\cap \infty}$ that ends at process $p_\ell \in D_\ell$, and is rooted at some process $q \in \mathcal{C}_q^\infty$ where $\mathcal{C}_q^\infty$ is a root component and thus by assumption not in D_ℓ. However, by the subgraph property (9.1), we know that the path Γ is also in $\mathcal{G}^{\cap r_\ell}$. But then Lemma 9.3.3 implies that $q \in G_{p_i}^{r_i}$, and Theorem 9.3.7 shows that

$$\mathcal{C}_q^\infty \in D_\ell,$$

i.e., one of the components in D_ℓ in fact *is* a root component, which provides a contradiction. □

By Theorem 9.2.1, at most k of the sets D_i can contain a root component, which directly contradicts Lemma 9.3.16. (Proof of Lemma 9.3.15)□

Tying together the results of this section yields the following theorem:

Theorem 9.3.17
Algorithm 6 solves k-set agreement in system $\mathcal{P}_{\mathrm{srcs}}(k)$.

Proof. Lemma 9.3.15 implies *k-agreement*. *Termination* is guaranteed by Lemma 9.3.10 and Lemma 9.3.8 shows *validity*. □

9.4. Discussion

The results of this chapter allow us to place the communication predicate $\mathcal{P}_{\mathrm{srcs}}(k)$ just above the models $\mathcal{M}^{\mathrm{anti}}$ and $\mathcal{M}^{\mathrm{sink}}$ in Figure 1.2 on Page 21. Note that for the case $n-1$, predicate $\mathcal{P}_{\mathrm{srcs}}(n-1)$ stipulates slightly stronger synchrony assumptions than the models of Chapter 6, since it requires the common source to be fixed throughout the run. Weakening this condition is part of our current research.

Throughout this chapter we have concentrated on k-set agreement in round-based systems. We now discuss how our results relate to other systems with up to $n-1$ crash failures. For the shared memory case, a class of partially synchronous system models was presented by Aguilera et al. (2009) recently, which allow to solve k-set agreement by implementing the corresponding weakest failure detector k-anti-Ω (see Gafni and Kuznetsov, 2009).

In Chapter 6 we have presented $\mathcal{M}^{\mathrm{sink}}$, which is a partially synchronous model where $(n-1)$-set agreement can be solved. That is, model $\mathcal{M}^{\mathrm{sink}}$ assumes that processes take steps in accordance with an upper bound on the relative process speeds. In contrast to Dolev et al. (1987); Dwork et al. (1988), however, there is no global bound on the maximum message delay in this model. Rather, we have used the notion of a timely link. In this spirit we can define the equivalent of a *2-source* of a set of processes S, by requiring that there are distinct processes $p_1, p_2 \in S$ such that the links from some process $p \in \Pi$ to p_1 and p_2 are timely; it may be that $p = p_1$ or $p = p_2$. If there is such a 2-source for any set of $k+1$ processes, we obtain a partially synchronous model $\mathcal{M}^{\mathrm{srcs}}(k)$ corresponding to $\mathcal{P}_{\mathrm{srcs}}(k)$.

With regard to our results from Chapter 7, a question that arises naturally is whether we can implement $\mathcal{L}(k)$ in such a model $\mathcal{P}_{\mathrm{srcs}}(k)$. We conjecture that this is impossible for $k < n-1$, since the ability to detect $n-k$ loneliness is a much stronger property (in particular for values of k close to 1) than the mere existence of a limited amount of timely links, as provided by $\mathcal{M}^{\text{srcs}}(k)$.

Appendix

List of Figures

1.1.	The space-time diagram of a run of a distributed system.	6
1.2.	The Space of System Models	21
3.1.	Relevant Cycle	31
3.2.	The Undirected Shadow Graph.	31
3.3.	Combined Relevant Cycle	32
3.4.	ABC Synchrony Condition	34
3.5.	A Non-Relevant Cycle	34
3.6.	An Asymmetric Relevant Cycle	38
3.7.	A Multi-Hop Relevant Cycle	39
3.8.	Bounded-Size FIFO Channel Implementation	40
4.1.	Proof of Lemma 4.1.6	50
5.1.	Matrix Form of the Linear System $\mathbf{Ax} < \mathbf{b}$.	66
5.2.	Cycle Vectors of a Relevant Cycle	68
6.1.	A Run in Model $\mathcal{M}^{\text{anti}}$	83
9.1.	The Stable Skeleton in Round 2	126
9.2.	The stable skeleton graph $\mathcal{G}^{\cap\infty}$	127
9.3.	The Approximation of the Stable Skeleton	132

List of Algorithms

1. Byzantine Clock Synchronization in the ABC Model 45
2. A Lock-Step Round Simulation Tolerating Byzantine Faults 54
3. Implementing $\mathcal{L}$ in Model $\mathcal{M}^{\text{anti}}$ 84
4. Implementing $\mathcal{L}$ in Model $\mathcal{M}^{\text{sink}}$ 87
5. Solving k-Set Agreement with $\mathcal{L}(k)$ 96
6. Approximating the Stable Skeleton Graph and Solving k-Set Agreement . 133

Bibliography

Aguilera, M. K., Delporte-Gallet, C., Fauconnier, H., and Toueg, S. (2001). Stable leader election. In *DISC '01: Proceedings of the 15th International Conference on Distributed Computing*, pages 108–122. Springer-Verlag.

Aguilera, M. K., Delporte-Gallet, C., Fauconnier, H., and Toueg, S. (2003). On implementing Omega with weak reliability and synchrony assumptions. In *Proceedings of the 22nd ACM Symposium on Principles of Distributed Computing*, pages 306–314, Boston, Massachusetts, USA.

Aguilera, M. K., Delporte-Gallet, C., Fauconnier, H., and Toueg, S. (2004). Communication-efficient leader election and consensus with limited link synchrony. In *Proceedings of the 23th ACM Symposium on Principles of Distributed Computing (PODC'04)*, pages 328–337, St. John's, Newfoundland, Canada. ACM Press.

Aguilera, M. K., Delporte-Gallet, C., Fauconnier, H., and Toueg, S. (2008). On implementing omega in systems with weak reliability and synchrony assumptions. *Distributed Computing*, 21(4).

Aguilera, M. K., Delporte-Gallet, C., Fauconnier, H., and Toueg, S. (2009). Partial synchrony based on set timeliness. In *PODC '09: Proceedings of the 28th ACM symposium on Principles of distributed computing*, pages 102–110, New York, NY, USA. ACM.

Akkoyunlu, E. A., Ekanadham, K., and Huber, R. V. (1975). Some constraints and tradeoffs in the design of network communications. In *SOSP '75: Proceedings of the fifth ACM symposium on Operating systems principles*, pages 67–74, New York, NY, USA. ACM.

Alpern, B. and Schneider, F. B. (1985). Defining liveness. *Information Processing Letters*, 21(4):181–185.

Anceaume, E., Fernández, A., Mostéfaoui, A., Neiger, G., and Raynal, M. (2004). A necessary and sufficient condition for transforming limited accuracy failure detectors. *J. Comput. Syst. Sci.*, 68(1):123–133.

Angluin, D. (1980). Local and global properties in networks of processors (extended abstract). In *Proceedings of the Twelfth Annual ACM Symposium on Theory of Computing*, pages 82–93. ACM.

Attiya, H., Dwork, C., Lynch, N., and Stockmeyer, L. (1994). Bounds on the time to reach agreement in the presence of timing uncertainty. *Journal of the ACM (JACM)*, 41(1):122–152.

Attiya, H., Snir, M., and Warmuth, M. K. (1988). Computing on an anonymous ring. *J. ACM*, 35(4):845–875.

Attiya, H. and Welch, J. (2004). *Distributed Computing: Fundamentals, Simulations and Advanced Topics (2nd ed.)*. John Wiley & Sons, Inc.

Ben-Zvi, I. and Moses, Y. (2010). Beyond lamport's happened-before: On the role of time bounds in synchronous systems. In Lynch, N. and Shvartsman, A., editors, *Distributed Computing*, volume 6343 of *Lecture Notes in Computer Science*, pages 421–436. Springer Berlin / Heidelberg.

Biely, M. and Hutle, M. (2009). Consensus when all processes may be byzantine for some time. In *Proceedings of the 11th International Symposium on Stabilization, Safety, and Security of Distributed Systems*, SSS '09, pages 120–132, Berlin, Heidelberg. Springer-Verlag.

Biely, M., Robinson, P., and Schmid, U. (2009a). Weak synchrony models and failure detectors for message passing k-set agreement. In *Proceedings of the International Conference on Principles of Distributed Systems (OPODIS'09)*, LNCS, pages 285–299, Nimes, France. Springer Verlag.

Biely, M., Robinson, P., and Schmid, U. (2009b). Weak synchrony models and failure detectors for message passing k-set agreement. In *Proceedings of the 23rd International Symposium on Distributed Computing (DISC'09)*, pages 260–261.

Biely, M., Robinson, P., and Schmid, U. (2010a). Solving k-set agreement with stable skeleton graphs. Research Report 28/2010, Technische Universität Wien, Institut für Technische Informatik, Treitlstr. 1-3/182-1, 1040 Vienna, Austria.

Biely, M., Robinson, P., and Schmid, U. (2011). Easy impossibility proofs for k-set agreement in message passing systems. Research Report 2/2011, Technische Universität Wien, Institut für Technische Informatik, Treitlstr. 1-3/182-1, 1040 Vienna, Austria.

Biely, M., Schmid, U., and Weiss, B. (2010b). Synchronous consensus under hybrid process and link failures. *Theoretical Computer Science*, In Press, Corrected Proof:–.

Biely, M. and Widder, J. (2006). Optimal message-driven implementation of Omega with mute processes. In *Proceedings of the Eighth International Symposium on Stabilization, Safety, and Security of Distributed Systems (SSS 2006)*, volume 4280 of *LNCS*, pages 110–121, Dallas, TX, USA. Springer Verlag.

Biely, M. and Widder, J. (2009). Optimal message-driven implementations of omega with mute processes. *ACM Transactions on Autonomous and Adaptive Systems*, 4(1):Article 4, 22 pages.

Bonnet, F. and Raynal, M. (2009). Looking for the weakest failure detector for k-set agreement in message-passing systems: Is Π_k the end of the road? In Guerraoui, R. and Petit, F., editors, *11th International Symposium on Stabilization, Safety, and Security of Distributed Systems (SSS 2009)*, volume 5873 of *Lecture Notes in Computer Science*, pages 129–164.

Bonnet, F. and Raynal, M. (2010a). Anonymous asynchronous systems: The case of failure detectors. In Lynch, N. and Shvartsman, A., editors, *Distributed Computing*, volume 6343 of *Lecture Notes in Computer Science*, pages 206–220. Springer Berlin / Heidelberg.

Bonnet, F. and Raynal, M. (2010b). On the road to the weakest failure detector for k-set agreement in message-passing systems. *Theoretical Computer Science*, In Press, Corrected Proof:–.

Borowsky, E. and Gafni, E. (1993). Generalized FLP impossibility result for t-resilient asynchronous computations. In *STOC '93: Proceedings of the twenty-fifth annual ACM symposium on Theory of computing*, pages 91–100, New York, NY, USA. ACM.

Bouzid, Z. and Travers, C. (2010). (Ω^x, Σ_z) based k-set agreement algorithms. In *OPODIS 2010*. Springer, Heidelberg. to appear.

Carver, W. B. (1921). Systems of linear inequalities. *Annals of Mathematics*, 23:212–220.

Chandra, T. D., Hadzilacos, V., and Toueg, S. (1996). The weakest failure detector for solving consensus. *Journal of the ACM*, 43(4):685–722.

Chandra, T. D. and Toueg, S. (1996). Unreliable failure detectors for reliable distributed systems. *Journal of the ACM*, 43(2):225–267.

Charron-Bost, B., Dolev, S., Ebergen, J., and Schmid, U., editors (2009). *Fault-Tolerant Distributed Algorithms on VLSI Chips*, Schloss Dagstuhl, Germany. http://drops.dagstuhl.de/opus/frontdoor.php?source_opus=1927.

Charron-Bost, B., Guerraoui, R., and Schiper, A. (2000). Synchronous system and perfect failure detector: Solvability and efficiency issues. In *Proceedings of the IEEE Int. Conf. on Dependable Systems and Networks (DSN'00)*, pages 523–532, New York, USA. IEEE Computer Society.

Charron-Bost, B. and Schiper, A. (2009). The Heard-Of model: computing in distributed systems with benign faults. *Distributed Computing*, 22(1):49–71.

Chaudhuri, S. (1993). More choices allow more faults: set consensus problems in totally asynchronous systems. *Inf. Comput.*, 105(1):132–158.

Delporte-Gallet, C., Fauconnier, H., and Guerraoui, R. (2010). Tight failure detection bounds on atomic object implementations. *J. ACM*, 57:22:1–22:32.

Delporte-Gallet, C., Fauconnier, H., Guerraoui, R., and Tielmann, A. (2008). The weakest failure detector for message passing set-agreement. In *DISC '08: Proceedings of the 22nd international symposium on Distributed Computing*, pages 109–120, Berlin, Heidelberg. Springer-Verlag.

Dielacher, A., Fuegger, M., and Schmid, U. (2009). Brief announcement: How to speed-up fault-tolerant clock generation in VLSI systems-on-chip via pipelining. In *Proceedings of the 28th ACM Symposium on Principles of Distributed Computing (PODC'09)*, page 423. ACM Press. An extended version is available as RR 15/2009, Institut für Technische Informatik, TU-Wien, http://www.vmars.tuwien.ac.at/documents/extern/2571/techreport.pdf.

Diestel, R. (2006). *Graph Theory (3rd ed.)*. Springer.

Dolev, D., Dwork, C., and Stockmeyer, L. (1987). On the minimal synchronism needed for distributed consensus. *Journal of the ACM*, 34(1):77–97.

Dolev, D., Halpern, J. Y., and Strong, H. R. (1986). On the possibility and impossibility of achieving clock synchronization. *Journal of Computer and System Sciences*, 32:230–250.

Dolev, D. and Strong, R. (1982). Distributed commit with bounded waiting. In *Proceedings of the 2nd Symposium on Reliability in Distributed Software and Database Systems,*, pages 53–60, Pittsburgh.

Dwork, C., Lynch, N., and Stockmeyer, L. (1988). Consensus in the presence of partial synchrony. *Journal of the ACM*, 35(2):288–323.

Ebergen, J. C. (1991). A formal approach to designing delay-insensitive circuits. *Distributed Computing*, 5:107–119.

Elrad, T. and Francez, N. (1982). Decomposition of distributed programs into communication-closed layers. *Science of Computer Programming*, 2(3):155–173.

Fernández, A., Jiménez, E., Raynal, M., and Trédan, G. (2010). A timing assumption and two t-resilient protocols for implementing an eventual leader service in asynchronous shared memory systems. *Algorithmica*, 56(4):550–576.

Fernández, A. and Raynal, M. (2007). From an intermittent rotating star to a leader. In *Proc. 11th Int'l Conference On Principles Of Distributed Systems (OPODIS'07)*, pages 189–203. Springer-Verlag.

Fernández, A. and Raynal, M. (2010). From an asynchronous intermittent rotating star to an eventual leader. *IEEE Trans. Parallel Distrib. Syst.*, 21(9):1290–1303.

Fetzer, C. (1998). The message classification model. In *Proceedings of the Seventeenth Annual ACM Symposium on Principles of Distributed Computing*, pages 153–162, Puerto Vallarta, Mexico. ACM Press.

Fetzer, C. and Schmid, U. (2004). Brief announcement: On the possibility of consensus in asynchronous systems with finite average response times. In *Proceedings of the 23th ACM Symposium on Principles of Distributed Computing (PODC'04)*, page 402, Boston, Massachusetts.

Fetzer, C., Schmid, U., and Süßkraut, M. (2005). On the possibility of consensus in asynchronous systems with finite average response times. In *Proceedings of the 25th International Conference on Distributed Computing Systems (ICDCS'05)*, pages 271–280, Washington, DC, USA. IEEE Computer Society.

Fischer, M. J., Lynch, N. A., and Paterson, M. S. (1985). Impossibility of distributed consensus with one faulty process. *Journal of the ACM*, 32(2):374–382.

Fuegger, M., Schmid, U., Fuchs, G., and Kempf, G. (2006). Fault-Tolerant Distributed Clock Generation in VLSI Systems-on-Chip. In *Proceedings of the Sixth European Dependable Computing Conference (EDCC-6)*, pages 87–96. IEEE Computer Society Press.

Gafni, E. (1998). Round-by-round fault detectors (extended abstract): unifying synchrony and asynchrony. In *Proceedings of the Seventeenth Annual ACM Symposium on Principles of Distributed Computing*, pages 143–152, Puerto Vallarta, Mexico. ACM Press.

Gafni, E. and Kuznetsov, P. (2009). The weakest failure detector for solving k-set agreement. In *28th ACM SIGACT-SIGOPS Symposium on Principles of Distributed Computing (PODC 2009)*.

Garcia-Molina, H. (1982). Elections in a distributed computing system. *IEEE Trans. Comput.*, 31(1):48–59.

Gray, J. N. (1978). Notes on data base operating systems. In R. Bayer, R.M. Graham, G. S., editor, *Operating Systems: An Advanced Course*, volume 60 of *Lecture Notes in Computer Science*, chapter 3.F, page 465. Springer, New York.

Guerraoui, R., Herlihy, M., Kouznetsov, P., Lynch, N., and Newport, C. (2007). On the weakest failure detector ever. In *Proceedings of the twenty-sixth annual ACM Symposium on Principles of Distributed Computing (PODC'07*, pages 235–243. ACM.

Guerraoui, R. and Schiper, A. (1996). "gamma-accurate" failure detectors. In *WDAG '96: Proceedings of the 10th International Workshop on Distributed Algorithms*, pages 269–286, London, UK. Springer-Verlag.

Hadzilacos, V. and Toueg, S. (1993). Fault-tolerant broadcasts and related problems. In Mullender, S., editor, *Distributed Systems*, chapter 5, pages 97–145. Addison-Wesley, 2nd edition.

Halpern, J. Y. and Moses, Y. (1990). Knowledge and common knowledge in a distributed environment. *J. ACM*, 37(3):549–587.

Herlihy, M. (1991). Wait-free synchronization. *ACM Transactions on Programming Language Systems*, 13(1):124–149.

Herlihy, M. and Shavit, N. (1993). The asynchronous computability theorem for t-resilient tasks. In *STOC '93: Proceedings of the twenty-fifth annual ACM symposium on Theory of computing*, pages 111–120, New York, NY, USA. ACM.

Hutle, M., Malkhi, D., Schmid, U., and Zhou, L. (2006). Brief announcement: Chasing the weakest system model for implementing omega and consensus. In *Proceedings Eighth International Symposium on Stabilization, Safety, and Security of Distributed Systems (SSS 2006)*, LNCS, pages 576–577, Dallas, USA. Springer Verlag.

Hutle, M., Malkhi, D., Schmid, U., and Zhou, L. (2009). Chasing the weakest system model for implementing omega and consensus. *IEEE Transactions on Dependable and Secure Computing*, 6(4):269–281.

Hutle, M. and Schiper, A. (2007). Communication predicates: A high-level abstraction for coping with transient and dynamic faults. In *37th Annual IEEE/IFIP International Conference on Dependable Systems and Networks (DSN'07)*, pages 92–101.

Imbs, D., Raynal, M., and Taubenfeld, G. (2010). On asymmetric progress conditions. In *PODC*, pages 55–64.

Jayanti, P. and Toueg, S. (2008). Every problem has a weakest failure detector. In *Proceedings of the twenty-seventh ACM symposium on Principles of distributed computing (PODC '08)*, pages 75–84, New York, NY, USA. ACM.

Kuhn, F., Lynch, N. A., and Oshman, R. (2010). Distributed computation in dynamic networks. In *STOC*, pages 513–522.

Lamport, L. (1978). Time, clocks, and the ordering of events in a distributed system. *Commun. ACM*, 21(7):558–565.

Lamport, L. and Melliar-Smith, P. M. (1985). Synchronizing clocks in the presence of faults. *Journal of the ACM*, 32(1):52–78.

Lamport, L., Shostak, R., and Pease, M. (1982). The Byzantine generals problem. *ACM Transactions on Programming Languages and Systems*, 4:382–401.

Lampson, B. W. and Sturgis, H. E. (1979). Crash recovery in a distributed data storage system.

Larrea, M., Fernández, A., and Arévalo, S. (2000). Optimal implementation of the weakest failure detector for solving consensus. In *Proceedings of the 19th IEEE Symposium on Reliable Distributed Systems (SRDS)*, pages 52–59, Nürnberg, Germany.

Le Lann, G. and Schmid, U. (2003). How to implement a timer-free perfect failure detector in partially synchronous systems. Technical Report 183/1-127, Department of Automation, Technische Universität Wien. (Replaced by Research Report 28/2005, Institut für Technische Informatik, TU Wien, 2005.).

Lynch, N. (1996). *Distributed Algorithms*. Morgan Kaufman Publishers, Inc., San Francisco, USA.

Lynch, N. A. and Fischer, M. J. (1979). On describing the behavior and implementation of distributed systems. In *Proceedings of the International Sympoisum on Semantics of Concurrent Computation*, pages 147–172, London, UK. Springer-Verlag.

Malkhi, D., Oprea, F., and Zhou, L. (2005). Ω meets paxos: Leader election and stability without eventual timely links. In *Proceedings of the 19th Symposium on Distributed Computing (DISC'05)*, volume 3724 of *LNCS*, pages 199–213, Cracow, Poland. Springer Verlag.

Malpani, N., Welch, J. L., and Vaidya, N. (2000). Leader election algorithms for mobile ad hoc networks. In *DIALM '00: Proceedings of the 4th international workshop on Discrete algorithms and methods for mobile computing and communications*, pages 96–103, New York, NY, USA. ACM.

Mattern, F. (1989). Virtual time and global states of distributed systems. In *Parallel and Distributed Algorithms*, pages 215–226. North-Holland.

Mattern, F. (1992). On the relativistic structure of logical time in distributed systems. In *Parallel and Distributed Algorithms*, pages 215–226. Elsevier Science Publishers B.V.

Moser, H. (2009). *A Model for Distributed Computing in Real-Time Systems*. PhD thesis, Technische Universität Wien, Fakultät für Informatik. (Promotion sub auspiciis).

Moser, H. and Schmid, U. (2006). Optimal clock synchronization revisited: Upper and lower bounds in real-time systems. In *Proceedings of the International Conference on Principles of Distributed Systems (OPODIS)*, LNCS 4305, pages 95–109, Bordeaux & Saint-Emilion, France. Springer Verlag.

Mostefaoui, A., Mourgaya, E., and Raynal, M. (2003). Asynchronous implementation of failure detectors. In *Proceedings of the International Conference on Dependable Systems and Networks (DSN'03)*, San Francisco, CA.

Mostéfaoui, A., Rajsbaum, S., Raynal, M., and Roy, M. (2002). Condition-based protocols for set agreement problems. In *DISC*, pages 48–62.

Mostéfaoui, A. and Raynal, M. (1999a). Solving consensus using Chandra-Toueg's unreliable failure detectors: A general quorum-based approach. In Jayanti, P., editor, *Distributed Computing: 13th International Symposium (DISC'99)*, volume 1693 of *Lecture Notes in Computer Science*, pages 49–63, Bratislava, Slovak Republic. Springer-Verlag GmbH.

Mostéfaoui, A. and Raynal, M. (1999b). Unreliable failure detectors with limited scope accuracy and an application to consensus. In *FSTTCS*, pages 329–340.

Mostéfaoui, A. and Raynal, M. (2000). k-set agreement with limited accuracy failure detectors. In *PODC '00: Proceedings of the 19th annual ACM symposium on Principles of distributed computing*, pages 143–152, New York, NY, USA. ACM.

Mostefaoui, A. and Raynal, M. (2001). Randomized k-set agreement. In *SPAA '01: Proceedings of the thirteenth annual ACM symposium on Parallel algorithms and architectures*, pages 291–297, New York, NY, USA. ACM.

Mostefaoui, A., Raynal, M., and Travers, C. (2004). Crash-resilient time-free eventual leadership. In *Proceedings of the 23rd IEEE Symposium on Reliable Distributed Systems (SRDS 2004)*, pages 208–217. IEEE Computer Society.

Neiger, G. (1995). Failure detectors and the wait-free hierarchy (extended abstract). In *Proceedings of the fourteenth annual ACM symposium on Principles of distributed computing*, PODC '95, pages 100–109, New York, NY, USA. ACM.

Pease, M., Shostak, R., and Lamport, L. (1980). Reaching agreement in the presence of faults. *Journal of the ACM*, 27(2):228–234.

Ponzio, S. and Strong, R. (1992). Semisynchrony and real time. In *Proceedings of the 6th International Workshop on Distributed Algorithms (WDAG'92)*, pages 120–135, Haifa, Israel.

Robinson, P. and Schmid, U. (2008a). The Asynchronous Bounded-Cycle Model. Research Report 24/2008, Technische Universität Wien, Institut für Technische Informatik, Treitlstr. 1-3/182-1, 1040 Vienna, Austria.

Robinson, P. and Schmid, U. (2008b). The Asynchronous Bounded-Cycle Model. In *Proceedings of the 10th International Symposium on Stabilization, Safety, and Security of Distributed Systems (SSS'08)*, volume 5340 of *Lecture Notes in Computer Science*, pages 246–262, Detroit, USA. Springer Verlag. (Best Paper Award).

Robinson, P. and Schmid, U. (2008c). Brief announcement: The asynchronous bounded-cycle model. In *Proceedings of the 27th ACM Symposium on Principles of Distributed Computing (PODC'08)*, page 423. ACM Press. (extended version appeared at SSS'08).

Robinson, P. and Schmid, U. (2010). The Asynchronous Bounded-Cycle Model. *Theoretical Computer Science*, 5340.

Saks, M. and Zaharoglou, F. (2000). Wait-free k-set agreement is impossible: The topology of public knowledge. *SIAM J. Comput.*, 29(5):1449–1483.

Santoro, N. and Widmayer, P. (1989). Time is not a healer. In *Proc. 6th Annual Symposium on Theor. Aspects of Computer Science (STACS'89)*, LNCS 349, pages 304–313, Paderborn, Germany. Springer-Verlag.

Sastry, S., Pike, S. M., and Welch, J. L. (2009). Crash fault detection in celerating environments. In *IPDPS '09: Proceedings of the 2009 IEEE International Symposium on Parallel&Distributed Processing*, pages 1–12, Washington, DC, USA. IEEE Computer Society.

Schmid, U. and Weiss, B. (2002). Synchronous Byzantine agreement under hybrid process and link failures. Technical Report 183/1-124, Department of Automation, Technische Universität Wien. (replaces TR 183/1-110).

Schmid, U., Weiss, B., and Keidar, I. (2009). Impossibility results and lower bounds for consensus under link failures. *SIAM Journal on Computing*, 38(5):1912–1951.

Sutherland, I. E. and Ebergen, J. (2002). Computers without Clocks. *Scientific American*, 287(2):62–69.

Taubenfeld, G. (2010). The computational structure of progress conditions. In Lynch, N. and Shvartsman, A., editors, *Distributed Computing*, volume 6343 of *Lecture Notes in Computer Science*, pages 221–235. Springer Berlin / Heidelberg.

Vitányi, P. M. (1984). Distributed elections in an archimedean ring of processors. In *Proceedings of the sixteenth annual ACM symposium on Theory of computing*, pages 542–547. ACM Press.

Vitányi, P. M. (1985). Time-driven algorithms for distributed control. Report CS-R8510, C.W.I.

Wagner, D. and Wattenhofer, R., editors (2007). *Algorithms for Sensor and Ad Hoc Networks, Advanced Lectures [result from a Dagstuhl seminar]*, volume 4621 of *Lecture Notes in Computer Science*. Springer.

Widder, J., Le Lann, G., and Schmid, U. (2005). Failure detection with booting in partially synchronous systems. In *Proceedings of the 5th European Dependable Computing Conference (EDCC-5)*, volume 3463 of *LNCS*, pages 20–37, Budapest, Hungary. Springer Verlag.

Widder, J. and Schmid, U. (2007). Booting clock synchronization in partially synchronous systems with hybrid process and link failures. *Distributed Computing*, 20(2):115–140.

Widder, J. and Schmid, U. (2009). The Theta-Model: Achieving synchrony without clocks. *Distributed Computing*, 22(1):29–47.

Die VDM Verlagsservicegesellschaft sucht für wissenschaftliche Verlage abgeschlossene und herausragende

Dissertationen, Habilitationen, Diplomarbeiten, Master Theses, Magisterarbeiten usw.

für die kostenlose Publikation als Fachbuch.

Sie verfügen über eine Arbeit, die hohen inhaltlichen und formalen Ansprüchen genügt, und haben Interesse an einer honorarvergüteten Publikation?

Dann senden Sie bitte erste Informationen über sich und Ihre Arbeit per Email an *info@vdm-vsg.de*.

Sie erhalten kurzfristig unser Feedback!

VDM Verlagsservicegesellschaft mbH
Dudweiler Landstr. 99　　　　　Telefon +49 681 3720 174
D - 66123 Saarbrücken　　　　　Fax　　　+49 681 3720 1749
www.vdm-vsg.de

Die VDM Verlagsservicegesellschaft mbH vertritt

MIX
Papier aus verantwortungsvollen Quellen
Paper from responsible sources
FSC® C105338

Printed by Books on Demand GmbH, Norderstedt / Germany